WORLD FAMOUS
UNSOLVED CRIMES

WORLD FAMOUS
UNSOLVED
CRIMES

Colin Wilson
with Damon and Rowan Wilson

SIENA

This is a Siena Book
Siena is an imprint of Parragon Book Service Ltd

Produced by Magpie Books, 1996
First published 1992 by Magpie Books
an imprint of Robinson Publishing, London
Copyright © 1992 Robinson Publishing

Cover pictures, Lord Lucan, Hulton Deutsch
The Black Dahlia, Popperfoto
Illustrations courtesy of Hulton Deutsch

British Library Cataloguing-in-Publication Data
A catalogue record for this book is available
from the British Library

ISBN 0 75251 627 2
10 9 8 7 6 5 4 3 2 1

Printed and Bound in the EC

Contents

Chapter One

Nineteenth-Century Unsolved Murders

An enormous percentage of murders — perhaps as many as one third — remain unsolved. This is particularly true in the late twentieth century, when "serial killers" strike at random — for example, in America in the 1980s, the uncaught "Green River Killer" of Seattle killed at least forty women, eight times as many as London's Jack the Ripper, who killed five prostitutes in 1888. So it is understandable that we look back on the nineteenth century with nostalgia, and find a certain quaint charm even in its murder cases. In fact, considering the undeveloped state of nineteenth-century crime detection, remarkably few of its famous murder cases remained unsolved.

One of the few that defied the skills of the New York police force was the case of the death of a salesgirl, which so intrigued Edgar Allen Poe that he used it as the basis for his story "The Mystery of Marie Roget".

If the death of "Marie Roget" is now no longer quite a mystery, the classic Victorian poisoning drama, the death of Charles Bravo, is as baffling as in 1876.

And another, the case of Lizzie Borden, is the most intriguing American murder mystery that took place almost a quarter of a century later, in 1892, and is regarded by most aficionados of crime as a fitting climax to the homicides of the age of gaslight.

The Case of Mary Rogers

Mary Cecilia Rogers was born in New York in 1820; her mother, who became a widow when the child was five, supported herself by running a boarding-house in Nassau Street. Mary grew up into a tall, very beautiful young woman with jet-black hair. This led a cigar-store owner named John Anderson, whose shop was on Broadway, to offer her a job as a salesgirl. In 1840 this was regarded as an imaginative piece of business enterprise, for New York was even more "Victorian" than London, and young unmarried girls did not exhibit themselves behind shop counters, particularly in shops frequented exclusively by young men. Mary's mother objected to the idea, but her daughter's enthusiasm finally won her over. She drew many new customers to the shop, although – as Thomas Duke is careful to note in his *Celebrated Criminal Cases of America* (1910) – "the girl's conduct was apparently a model of modest decorum, and while she was lavish in her smiles, she did not hesitate to repel all undue advances".

She had been working in the store for about ten months when one day in January 1841 she failed to appear. Her mother had no idea where she was, and according to Duke, "Mr Anderson was unable to account for her absence". The police searched for her and the newspapers reported her disappearance. Six days later she reappeared, looking tired and rather ill, and explained that she had been visiting relatives in the country. Her mother and her employer apparently corroborated the story. But when a rumour began to circulate that she had been seen during her absence with a tall, handsome naval officer Mary abruptly gave up her job – only a few days after returning – and was no longer seen on Broadway. A month later she announced her engagement to one of her mother's boarders, a clerk called Daniel Payne.

Five months later, on Sunday, 25 July 1841, Mary knocked on her fiancé's door at 10 a.m. and announced that she was going to see her aunt in Bleecker Street; Payne said that he would call for her that evening. Payne also spent the day away from home, but when a violent thunderstorm came on towards evening he decided not to call for Mary, but to let her stay the night with her aunt. Mrs Rogers apparently approved. But when Mary failed to return home the following day she began to worry. When Payne returned from work and learned that Mary was still away, he rushed to see the aunt in Bleecker Street — a Mrs Downing — and was even more alarmed when she told him that she had not seen Mary in the past forty-eight hours.

It was two days later on Wednesday morning that three men in a sailing-boat saw a body in the water off Castle Point, Hoboken. It was Mary, and according to the *New York Tribune* "it was obvious that she had been horribly outraged and murdered". She was fully clothed, although her clothes were torn, and the petticoat was missing. A piece of lace from the bottom of the dress was embedded so deeply in the throat that it had almost disappeared. An autopsy performed almost immediately led to the conclusion that she had been "brutally violated". Oddly enough, Daniel Payne did not go to view the corpse, although he had earlier searched for her all over New York, including Hoboken. But after being interrogated by the police, Payne was released.

A week passed without any fresh clues, and a large reward was offered. Then the coroner received a letter from some anonymous man — who said he had not come forward before from "motives of perhaps criminal prudence" — and who claimed to have seen Mary Rogers on the Sunday afternoon of her disappearance. She had, the writer said, stepped out of a boat with six rough-looking characters, and gone with them into the woods, laughing merrily and apparently under no kind of constraint. Soon afterwards a boat with three well-dressed men had come ashore, and one of these accosted two men walking on the beach and asked if they had seen a young woman and six men recently. They said they had, and that she had appeared to go with them willingly. At this the trio turned their boat and headed back for New York.

In fact, the two men came forward and corroborated this story. But although they both knew Mary Rogers by sight, neither of them could swear that the girl they had seen was definitely Mary.

The next important piece of information came from a stagecoach-driver named Adams, who said he had seen Mary arrive on the Hoboken ferry with a well-dressed man of dark complexion, and that they had gone to a roadhouse called "Nick Mullen's". This tavern was kept by a Mrs Loss, who told the police that the couple had "taken refreshment" there, then gone off into the woods. Some time later she had heard a scream from the woods; but since the place "was a resort of questionable characters" she had thought no more of it.

Two months after the murder, on 25 September, children playing in the woods found the missing petticoat in a thicket; they also found a white silk scarf, a parasol and a handkerchief marked "M.R.". Daniel Payne was to commit suicide in this spot soon after.

A gambler named Joseph Morse, who lived in Nassau Street, was arrested and apparently charged with the murder; there was evidence that he had been seen with Mary Rogers on the evening she disappeared. The following day, he had fled from New York. But Morse was released when he was able to prove that he had been at Staten Island with another young lady on the Sunday afternoon. One odd story in the *Tribune* declared that Morse believed that the young lady *was* Mary Rogers, and that when he heard of the disappearance he assumed she had committed suicide because of the way he had treated her — he had tried to seduce her in his room. He was relieved to learn that the girl with whom he had spent the afternoon was still alive.

In the following year, 1842, Poe's "Mystery of Marie Roget" was published in three parts in *Snowden's Ladies' Companion*. But for anyone looking for a solution of the Mary Rogers mystery, it should be treated with extreme caution. Poe argues that Mary Rogers was not murdered by a gang but by a single individual. His original view seems to have been that the motive was rape; later he heard the rumour that Mary had died as a result of an abortion, and made a few hasty alterations in his story to accommodate this notion. He argues that the signs of a struggle in the woods, and the battered state of her face, indicate that she was killed by an individual — a gang would have been able to overpower her easily. He also speaks of a strip from the girl's skirt that had been wound around the waist to afford a kind of handle for carrying the body; but the evidence of two witnesses who dragged the body out of the water makes no mention of this "handle". In spite of this, there can be no doubt that Poe's objections to the gang theory carry a great deal of weight.

What was not known to Poe in 1842 is that Mary's employer, John Anderson, had been questioned by the police as a suspect; like all the others, he was released. But fifty years later — in December 1891 — new evidence was to emerge. By that time Anderson had been dead ten years; he became a millionaire, and died in Paris. Apparently he had told friends that he had experienced "many unhappy days and nights in regard to her" (Mary Rogers), and had been in touch with her spirit. His heirs contested his estate, and in 1891 his daughter tried to break her father's will on the grounds that when he signed it he was mentally incompetent. The case was settled out of court, and the records destroyed. But a lawyer named Samuel Copp Worthen,

> The early "bobbies" wore top hats lined with steel — not to protect their heads in case of attack, but so that they could stand on them if looking over a wall or through a window at head level.

who had been closely associated with Anderson's daughter Laura Appleton, knew that his firm had kept a copy of the testimony in the Supreme Court of New York in 1891, and he made it his business to read it. He finally revealed what he had learned in the periodical *American Literature* in 1948. It revealed that Anderson had been questioned by the police about the death of Mary Rogers, and that this had preyed on his mind, so that he later declined to stand as a candidate for mayor of New York, in case someone revealed his secret.

The most significant part of the testimony was the assertion that Anderson had admitted to paying for an abortion for Mary Rogers and had got "in some trouble over it". But he had insisted that he had not "had anything, directly, himself to do with her problems".

This would obviously explain Mary's week-long disappearance from the cigar store, and the fact that she looked tired and ill when she returned. It probably also explains why she decided to leave the store a week later — not because of gossip about the naval officer, but because she needed more time to convalesce.

Worthen's theory is that in the six months after leaving the cigar store Mary again got herself pregnant, and once more appealed to Anderson for help. When she left home that Sunday morning she intended to go to Hoboken for an abortion. (In fact, there was a story that Mrs Loss, the tavern-owner, had admitted on her deathbed that Mary Rogers had died during an abortion; there is no hard evidence for this confession, but it *is* known that the District Attorney was inclined to the abortion theory of Mary's death.) She died during the abortion, and her body was dumped in the river to protect the abortionist — the dark-skinned man with whom she was seen on the ferry — and Mrs Loss's family.

How does this theory fit the known facts? The answer is: very well indeed, particularly if we make the natural assumption that the father of the second unborn child was Daniel Payne — for it seems unlikely that Mary agreed to marry him, then continued her affair with her former lover. (Nothing is known about this former lover, but Anderson is obviously a suspect.) We must assume, then, that Payne knew perfectly well that Mary was on her way to Hoboken to have an illegal operation. We may also probably assume that the pregnancy was still in its early stages, and that Mary anticipated very little trouble — after all, she had recovered from the earlier abortion in a week, though it still left her feeling ill. Mary's mother was probably also in on the secret. Duke comments: "It was generally believed at the time that the murdered girl's mother knew more about her daughter's mysterious admirer than she chose to tell."

What of the evidence about the gang? It is possible, of course, that a young girl was actually seen entering the woods with a gang of men, and that this was nothing to do with Mary Rogers. But it is far more probable that the anonymous letter claiming that Mary had entered the woods with six ruffians was sent by Mrs Loss or one of her friends — it came from Hoboken. Then all she had to do was to persuade two of her relatives or friends to claim that they were the men on the beach, and that they had seen Mary enter the woods and seen the boat with three men that landed shortly afterwards . . . The result would be a perfect red herring, directing the attention of the police away from her own abortion parlour.

Unsolved Crimes

What of the petticoat found later in the woods? This, significantly enough, was found by Mrs Loss's children. We may assume that the petticoat, the umbrella and the handkerchief were left behind in Mrs Loss's roadhouse when Mary's body was dragged to the water in the middle of the night, and were later planted in the woods, in a place where the bushes were broken, to suggest evidence of a struggle.

And what of the evidence that Mary had been raped? This, apparently, was the coroner's report; we do not know whether she was examined by a doctor or if so what the doctor concluded. What we *do* know is that Mary's body was already decomposing, and that because of the hot July weather it was buried within a few hours of being taken out of the water; so any inquest would have been performed in haste. In 1841 the science of legal medicine was in its infancy, and it is doubtful whether anyone took a vaginal swab and examined it under a microscope for spermatozoa. What was probably taken for evidence of rape was actually evidence of an abortion that had gone wrong.

Duke reports that Daniel Payne committed suicide "at the same spot in the woods where his sweetheart was probably slain". Other writers on the case have questioned this (notably Charles E. Pearce in *Unsolved Murder Mysteries*, 1924). But Payne's suicide would certainly be consistent with the theory that he was the father of the unborn child.

It is a disappointing — if obvious — solution to one of the great "murder mysteries", that Mary Rogers died in the course of an abortion. Why is it not more generally known? Partly because Poe himself obscured the truth. In the 1850 edition of Poe's works published the year after his death, "Marie Roget" appeared with a footnote that stated:

> It may not be improper to record . . . that the confessions of *two* persons (one of them the Madame

> In a magazine called *The Unexplained* (No. 152),
> Grahame Fuller and Ian Knight suggest that Poe
> himself may have been the killer of Mary
> Rogers. A witness said he had seen her with a
> tall, well-dressed man of swarthy complexion on
> the afternoon she died; Poe was of olive
> complexion, and was always well-dressed. But
> he was only five feet eight inches tall. Poe's
> biographers all insist on his gentleness and
> courtesy. On the whole, the notion of Poe as a
> demonic killer, writing "Marie Roget" to boast
> about his crime, must be relegated to the realm
> of fantasy.

Dulac of the narrative [Mrs Loss]) made at different
periods long subsequent to the publication confessed,
in full, not only the general conclusion but absolutely
all the chief hypothetical details by which the conclusion was attained.

But this is obviously impossible. Mrs Loss only seems to
have confessed that Mary had died in the course of an
abortion in her tavern. Poe's theory was that she was
murdered by a man "in a passion" who then dragged her
body to the seashore. The likely truth seems to be that
she died of an air embolism, and that the abortionist,
with the aid of Mrs Loss, made the death look like
murder by tying a strip of cloth round her throat; the
two of them then probably carried it to the water. Poe's
"Marie Roget", far from being an amazingly accurate
reconstruction of the murder, is simply a bad guess. Poe
may not have been a murderer, but he was undoubtedly
a liar.

The Bravo Case

It happened in the Priory, Balham, south London, where Charles Bravo, a thirty-year-old barrister, lived with his newly-married wife Florence. She was an attractive girl, who had been a widow for four years when Bravo married her in December 1875. Her first husband, Captain Alexander Lewis Ricardo, of the Grenadier Guards, had died of alcoholism, leaving Florence a welcome — and, she thought, well-earned — £40,000.

When Charles Bravo proposed to her, he was aware that she was the mistress of a middle-aged doctor called James Manby Gully, who had tended her when her first marriage was breaking up. Charles's sexual past had not been entirely blameless, so the lovers agreed to put all thoughts of jealousy from their minds. Charles was undoubtedly in love with her, and just as undoubtedly attracted by her money.

As she soon discovered, he could be overbearing and bad-tempered; but Florence wasn't the type to be bullied. She had a mind of her own — and a tendency to drink rather too heavily. She ran the Priory — an imposing Gothic pile — with the help of a widow named Mrs Cox. To begin with, the marriage seemed happy — even though Florence had two miscarriages in four months, and Bravo suffered from fits of retrospective fury about Gully, and once even struck her.

On Friday, 21 April 1876, Charles Bravo ate a good supper of whiting, roast lamb, and anchovy eggs on toast, washing it down with burgundy. Florence and Mrs Cox drank most of two bottles of sherry between them. At ten that night, loud groans came from Bravo's bedroom; he had been seized with severe abdominal pains, and began vomiting. He vomited for three days, until he died.

Sir William Gull, Queen Victoria's physician (who was suspected by some twentieth-century criminologists of

Charles Bravo.

being Jack the Ripper), saw him before he died, and gave his opinion that Bravo was suffering from some irritant poison. A post-mortem confirmed this — there were signs of antimony poisoning. At this point Mrs Cox declared that Bravo had told her: "I have taken poison. Don't tell Florence."

An open verdict was returned at the inquest. But the newspapers smelled scandal, and openly hinted that Florence had killed her husband. Another inquest was held, prompted by Charles's brother Joseph, who was out to get a verdict of wilful murder — which would lead to Florence's arrest.

This time, the Dr Gully scandal came into open court — doing Gully a great deal of professional damage. Added to this, a dismissed servant of the Bravos' testified that he had once bought tartar emetic for the doctor. But again, the jury decided that there was not enough evidence to charge anyone — although they agreed that it *was* a case of murder. So Florence was exculpated, and she died of alcoholism two years later in Southsea.

Ever since then, students of crime have argued about the case. The most popular theory, obviously, is that Florence did it. An inquest on the body of her first husband — conducted after the Bravo inquest — showed traces of antimony in *his* organs. However, Ricardo had by then been separated from Florence for months.

It seems possible that his violent attacks of vomiting were not due to alcoholism, but to slow poisoning with antimony. But why should Florence kill her husband? Possibly because he insisted on his marital rights, and she was terrified of further miscarriages; possibly because she came to realize that he was interested only in her money.

In *How Charles Bravo Died*, author Yseult Bridges suggests that Bravo accidentally took the poison with which he had been dosing Florence. Crime novelist Agatha

Florence Bravo.

The enquiry into the Bravo case.

Christie believed that Dr Gully did it, or helped Florence to do it. Many other writers believe Mrs Cox was the culprit. Bravo disliked her, and is known to have wanted to get rid of her. The Priory has now been turned into working-class flats, and has a reputation for being haunted; but no one has ever produced a satisfactory explanation of the mystery of Bravo's death.

Lizzie Borden

At 11.15, on the morning of 4 August 1892 — the hottest day of the year — Lizzie Borden called the maid Bridget Sullivan and told her that someone had killed her father. The seventy-year-old banker was found on the divan in the parlour, his face unrecognizable; someone had struck him several blows with a hatchet. Borden's second wife, Abby, was believed to be out visiting a sick friend — according to Lizzie — but she was later found upstairs in the guest room, lying face downwards. She had also been killed with blows from a hatchet — much heavier, more savage blows than those that had killed Andrew Borden. Lizzie's story was that she had been out in the barn, and had heard a cry from the house; she rushed back to find her father dead.

It soon became clear that Lizzie had much to hide. Her mother had died when she was two; two years later her father remarried; Abby Gray was six years his junior, twenty-two years older than Lizzie's sister Emma. Two days before the murder, Lizzie had tried to buy prussic acid. Lizzie's father and stepmother had been experiencing stomach pains for some time before the murder. Lizzie hated her stepmother.

Moreover, medical evidence proved that Abby Borden had died shortly after 9 a.m., while her husband was not killed until about two hours later. It was just within the bounds of possibility that an unknown assassin had entered the house and murdered the couple — but not that he had remained concealed for two hours, in a small house in which there were two women. (Lizzie's sister was away staying with friends.)

Lizzie was arrested and tried. The evidence against her was purely circumstantial; the prosecution merely attempted to demonstrate that she was the likeliest person to have committed the murders. But she was a respectable girl of unblemished reputation, and the jury found her not guilty. She lived on until 1927. During her lifetime it was impossible for writers to speculate about whether she killed her father and stepmother. But after her death, Edmund Pearson lost no time in publishing his opinion that she was the killer. (Even during her lifetime, the local newspaper in Fall River, Massachusetts, printed sarcastic articles on the anniversary of the murder — one of which concluded that the Bordens had not been murdered at all, but had died of the heat.) His *Trial of Lizzie Borden* in the Great American Trial series, came out in 1937, and the book is dedicated to the district attorney who built up the case against Lizzie Borden. In 1959, a new piece of evidence turned up. In a book called *Murder and Mutiny*, published in 1959, E. R. Snow tells how he received a letter from an elderly gentleman named Thomas Owens, who had listened to a broadcast about the Borden case by Snow. Owens had a strange story to tell. In 1896, four years after the murder, Lizzie Borden went into the art gallery and shop of Tilden-Thurber in Providence, Rhode Island, and when she left, the assistant found that two expensive paintings on porcelain were missing. The following February, a lady went into the shop with one of the two paintings, and asked if a crack could be repaired. The manager was told, and he asked the lady where she had obtained the painting. "From Miss Lizzie Borden of Fall River." As a result of this, a headline "Lizzie Again" appeared in the *Providence Journal*, which stated that a warrant for her arrest had been issued for the theft of two paintings. What had happened, said Owens, was that the owners of the gallery had put a proposition to Lizzie: sign a confession to the murders, or we prosecute. Lizzie refused, and the item was published in the newspaper. This caused Lizzie to change her mind. After promises that the confession would not be used, Lizzie typed on a sheet of paper: "Unfair means force my signature here admitting the act of August 4, 1892, as mine alone, Lizbeth A Borden." The store decided to have the document photographed in case of accident, and Owens was asked to do it. He did; but he also made a second copy — or, he said, decided that the first copy was indistinct, and made another one for the store, without mentioning that he had the other. As the four principals in the episode died — there were two other men besides the store owners — he expected it to be publicized. And now, Owens was willing to sell the photograph of Lizzie's confessions for one hundred dollars. Snow persuaded him to take fifty, and printed the story in his book.

Another crime writer, Edward Radin, decided to look into the matter, and he soon established that Snow had been the victim of a swindler. It was Lizzie's signature, and the type face was that of a machine of the period, but the signature had been traced from Lizzie's will. It would be interesting to know whether Mr Snow demanded his fifty dollars back.

But obviously, the first part of the story was true. Lizzie *had* stolen the paintings, and the item really appeared in the *Providence Journal* in February 1897. Lizzie was a kleptomaniac. Although she had plenty of money (she left over a million dollars), she was a compulsive stealer. Oddly enough, she was also capable of great generosity.

Radin's book *Lizzie Borden, The Untold Story* asserts that Lizzie was innocent. The killer was Bridget Sullivan, the servant girl. It is known that Bridget was feeling ill on the morning of 4 August; yet Mrs Borden had her cleaning all the outside windows at 7.30 in the morning. Later that morning, Bridget vomited. Certainly, she had a motive of sorts — sheer resentment at her employer. Radin tells how he was completely convinced by Pearson's view of the case until he read the actual trial reports for himself and discovered that Pearson had suppressed many pieces of evidence in Lizzie's favour.

In 1964, Gerald Gross edited a volume of selections from Edmund Pearson's articles on murder, and wrote a postscript to Pearson's "final word" on the Borden case. Gross

LIEZIE BORDEN.   EMMA BORDEN.   REV. MR. BUCK. MRS. C. J. HOLMES.   MR. C. J. HOLMES.
THE PRISONER AND HER FRIENDS IN COURT.

Lizzie Borden in court.

says, very fairly, that Radin has distorted the evidence for Lizzie's innocence as carefully as Pearson distorted that for her guilt, and he points out that Pearson had to do a great deal of omitting anyway, to pack the trial into one fair-sized volume. But Gross's theory is that Lizzie killed her parents aided and abetted by Bridget. There is a persistent story that Bridget returned to Ireland after the trial, with a great deal of money given to her by Lizzie. Radin points out, quite correctly, that Bridget could certainly not be said to have testified in Lizzie's favour at the trial; on the contrary, most of her evidence told against her employer. If, however, she was an accomplice — or an accessory after the fact — perhaps to helping Lizzie conceal the murder weapon or the bloodstained dress (which Lizzie burnt) — then Lizzie would certainly have a motive for giving her money.

In 1967 there appeared in America, Victoria Lincoln's *A Private Disgrace*. When Foster Damon — another expert on the Borden case — sent me a copy, he enclosed a card which said: "I think this is the final word on Lizzie." I am inclined to think he is right.

Victoria Lincoln was born in Fall River, so her insight into the town is obviously authentic. She was able to uncover some facts that suddenly make the whole case quite clear. There is only one point in Miss Lincoln's account that might be described as "speculation"; from accounts of the periodic fainting illness that Lizzie suffered from, she arrives at the conclusion that Lizzie suffered from epilepsy of the temporal lobe of the brain. Psychomotor epilepsy is distinguished by seizures of automatic activity. Miss Lincoln cites a case from a medical textbook in which a man woke from a seizure, to find that the boss had raised his salary, impressed by the lucid and forceful way in which the man had asked for a raise. Lizzie undoubtedly had strange attacks about four times a year, always at the time of her menstrual period. The evidence about these attacks points to psychomotor epilepsy. And Lizzie was menstruating at the time of the murders.

But Miss Lincoln's theory is not an attempt to prove that Lizzie committed the murders in a trance-like state. She intended to kill her stepmother — but by poison. She hated her and was violently jealous of her. A year before the murders, her stepmother's room had been broken into and robbed when Lizzie was in the house. The thief was supposed to have flitted in silently, without alerting Lizzie, Emma and the maid Bridget, broken into the room, taken money and jewellery, and flitted out via the cellar door. Andrew Borden soon asked the police to drop the investigation. He had a fairly shrewd idea of the identity of the thief.

Lizzie felt she had reason for hating her stepmother. First of all, it was a quarrel about a house. Mrs Borden's sister had not married so well, and she lived in half a house, the other half of which belonged to her mother. Her mother wanted to sell, but could hardly turn her own daughter out. So

Andrew Borden came to the rescue, and quietly bought the whole house, giving half to the sister, and half to his own wife Abby. He did this with great secrecy, knowing the feelings of his children about their stepmother and her family, but the news leaked. Lizzie was furious. She told her father that charity should begin at home. She ceased to call Abby "mother", and from then on, addressed her — when she had to — as Mrs Borden. Andrew Borden tried to restore peace in the home by giving Lizzie and her sister another house, which had belonged to their grandfather. Lizzie was placated; but she never forgave her stepmother, and continued to address her as "Mrs Borden" after twenty-three years of calling her "mother".

The trouble that led directly to the murder was an identical situation, which took place five years later — just before the murder. Uncle John Vinnicum Morse was a mid-westerner, and he decided that he would like to move closer to his brother-in-law's home (he was the brother of Borden's first wife). Borden owned a farm at nearby Swansea, and Morse asked if he could rent it. Borden said yes — and decided to do again what he had already done over the business of his sister-in-law's house — to transfer the farm to his wife's name. Miss Lincoln dug up this curious transaction, the immediate motive of the murder; Pearson and the other writers on the case were unaware of it. Lizzie already disliked Uncle John because he had aided and abetted her father in the previous house transaction. So now he moved into their house again as a guest, she felt distinctly edgy. Miss Lincoln does not produce a convincing explanation why Borden decided to transfer the farm to Abby; perhaps he wanted to give her a present — he had recently bought back the other house from his daughters for two thousand more than its value, thus making them a present of a thousand dollars each. But Borden was seventy; no doubt he wanted to leave his wife well provided for in the event of his death. This was also why Lizzie was so bitterly opposed to these property deals. And it did not take long for the news about the Swansea property to leak back to her. This is when she started trying to buy poison. And although she was unsuccessful in her attempts to buy prussic acid ("for cleaning a fur"), she presumably bought *something*, for that evening Mr and Mrs Borden were very sick indeed. Lizzie said she had been sick too, but we have only her word for this.

There was another factor that has been largely ignored by Pearson and Radin. Lizzie had a deep love of animals, and she owned some pigeons, which lived in the barn roost. Borden kept everything locked up – he was capable of obsessive meanness – and when the barn was broken into twice by youths who wanted pigeon pie for supper, he chopped off the heads of all the pigeons with a hatchet. It was not exactly unkindness; in those days, America was still close to the pioneers, and most people killed their own chickens and butchered their own hogs. But he failed to calculate the effect on Lizzie.

This, in summary, is the new evidence dug up by Victoria Lincoln, and it certainly makes the case in every way more straightforward. The transfer of the deeds on the Swansea property was to take place on the day of the murder. Borden had thought up a stratagem to do this without arousing Lizzie's suspicions – a carriage would be sent to the door, and a note requesting that Mrs Borden visit a sick neighbour. The note arrived – or so Miss Lincoln believes – but by then, Mrs Borden was already dead, or about to die. She was working in the guest room, on all fours, when Lizzie came in behind her with the hatchet, and sliced into her skull with blow after blow. At this point, Miss Lincoln embarks on a speculation that I find difficult to accept. John Morse had left the house much earlier. He had no alibi for the time of the first murder, but an extremely detailed one for the second. Miss Lincoln believes that Morse went along to the house just to make sure that all went according to plan — after all, the affair of the farm was of immediate interest to him. He watched the boy deliver the note, and observed Lizzie's very abrupt manner as she took it, followed by her slamming of the door. Obviously, she was having one of her queer spells. Ever since Morse had been in the Bordens' house, there had been a brooding tension, and Mrs Borden probably suspected Lizzie of wanting to poison her. So Morse listened with more than usual attention to what followed, and rightly interpreted the heavy thud from the upstairs room — its window was wide open on the hot August morning — followed by a succession of squelching noises. Probably Mrs Borden groaned the first time — Bridget was out at the other side of the house cleaning windows, so she would not hear. And Morse, realizing what had happened, knew that an uncle from the mid-west would be a far more likely suspect for a murder than the respectable daughter of the house. So he hurried away and started establishing an alibi.

This *could* have happened, but there is no evidence that it did. All that seems moderately certain is that, with the stifling heat of the August morning, and the irritation of her menstrual period, Lizzie had one of her queer spells, and decided that she could not stand her step-mother a moment longer. Miss Lincoln may well be right; it may have been committed in a dream-like state, and the dream may have involved the headless pigeons. Miss Lincoln could be wrong in her diagnosis of psychomotor epilepsy; but it is hard to doubt that all kinds of factors — the knowledge of another property deal, her hatred of her stepmother and determination to kill her, the heat, menstrual irritation — suddenly decided her to use violence. Earlier writers on the case were not aware of just *how much* violence and tension there was in the air in the Borden house in the weeks before the murder; it was a storm that had to break. Borden broke his usual habit of reticence to tell a business associate that he was having a lot of trouble at home at the moment.

What Lizzie did about her bloodstained dress after this first murder is rather a mystery. Presumably she took it off. At 10.45, Andrew Borden arrived home unexpectedly, no doubt puzzled by his wife's non-appearance at the bank. His daughter was on the point of leaving the house — to establish an alibi. The doors were locked — as usual — and Bridget had to let him in. Lizzie was heard to give a strange laugh as her father came in. She told her father that Mrs Borden had been called away to see a sick neighbour. Possibly Andrew Borden accepted this story; possibly he supposed Mrs Borden and Uncle John were now signing papers that he had already signed. At all events, he went into the sitting room and fell asleep. Bridget Sullivan testified that he was carrying "something like a book". Miss Lincoln is inclined to believe that this "something" wrapped in white paper was the deeds to the Swansea property, and the agreement to transfer it. Lizzie was later seen burning something in the kitchen stove.

What happened next? Miss Lincoln believes that Lizzie genuinely loved her father, but that seeing him asleep, was tempted to spare him the horror of seeing his wife's body, and knowing that Lizzie was the killer. (For he *would* have known, just as he knew that Lizzie was the invisible thief of a year earlier.) Undoubtedly, he loved her, and he would cease to do so when the body was discovered. And so, according to Miss Lincoln, she regretfully raised the hatchet. . . .

I find this hard to accept. Andrew Borden was killed with nine blows, one of which sliced through his eye. Lizzie must have gone back upstairs to change her dress before the murder — unless she disposed of two bloodstained dresses — and then gone to get the hatchet from the basement. (It is true that she may have kept the dress in the basement too.) Two days before, her father had suffered from the same serious stomach complaint as her stepmother. She had made up her mind to kill him too. She did it less violently than in the case of her stepmother — nine blows instead of seventeen — but unflinchingly. Then she went to the barn and washed the hatchet, smashed off its bloodstained handle in a vice — which she burnt — and rubbed the blade in ashes. She removed the dress and folded it into a bundle. Or she may have simply hung it in her closet among her other dresses, as Miss Lincoln suggests, simply putting it inside another. By the time Bridget came in from cleaning the windows, and went to her room to lie down for a moment, Lizzie had changed and was ready to give the alarm.

There is some evidence for the epilepsy theory. Lizzie's mother suffered from severe migraines and sudden violent seizures of unmotivated rage. The evening before the murder, Lizzie called on a friend, Alice Russell, and said: "I'm afraid someone will do something. I don't know what but someone will do something." The heat wave had started the day before; she was experiencing the sense of brooding depression that Dostoievsky has described as preceding epileptic fits. "I feel depressed," she told Miss Russell, "I feel as if something was hanging over me that I can't shake off." Only that morning there had been a strange scene; her stepmother had approached a Doctor Bowen who lived opposite, and told him that her husband had received a letter threatening to poison him, and that they had been sick all the previous night. Doctor Bowen finally agreed to come to the house — and was met by a furious Andrew Borden, who told him to mind his own business and go away. And meanwhile the heat was tremendous, oppressive — it was one of the hottest days recorded in Fall River in living memory — and Lizzie's abdomen was aching in a way that indicated the approach of a menstrual period . . . She may well have foreboding.

No, forensic medicine would have made no difference to the Borden case. It might have established blood on the blade of the ash-coated hatchet, and drawn the net of circumstantial evidence a little tighter. And if someone had had Miss Lincoln's shrewdness, the forensic laboratories might have examined the *inside* of all Lizzie Borden's dresses for bloodstains that proved that a bloodstained dress had been hung up inside one of them. For what Lizzie did with the bloodstained dress between the day of the murder — Thursday — and Sunday morning, when she burnt it, is the chief unsolved mystery of the case. Emma and Alice Russell walked into the kitchen, and interrupted Lizzie, who was holding the Bedford cord dress. "I'm going to burn this old thing," said Lizzie. "It's all covered up with paint." Alice and Emma must have exchanged a horrified glance. It was their moment of decision. If they snatched it from Lizzie, or casually asked to look at it, it would undoubtedly send Lizzie to the scaffold. But what was the point? The Bordens were dead, and both Emma and her friend Alice knew about Lizzie's "queer spells". Alice merely said: "I wouldn't let anyone see you doing that if I were you," and then conveniently forgot the incident for four months. When Alice was questioned about Lizzie's dresses the next day, she went in to Lizzie and told her she really ought not to have burnt the dress. Lizzie simulated concern, and said: "Why did you let me do it?" Quite.

Was it the Ripper?

Elliott O'Donnell's book *Great Thames Mysteries* (1929) contains a chapter called 'Was it Jack the Ripper?' It begins: 'In May 1887 began a series of mysterious crimes which, for barbarity and almost superhuman cunning, have rarely been equalled and certainly surpassed.'

He describes how two men pulled a bundle out of the river at Rainham, in Essex, and found that it contained the trunk of a woman of about 28, with the head, arms and legs missing.

On 8 June, 1887, another parcel was found in the Thames near Temple Stairs and proved to contain some of the limbs that belonged to the previous body. More remains found in Regent's Canal, Chalk Farm, also proved to belong to the body. At the inquest, the pathologist declared that the limbs had been severed by someone with a knowledge of anatomy.

On 11 September, 1888 — the year of the Jack the Ripper murders — an arm was found in the Thames near Pimlico, and two weeks later, another arm in the grounds of the Blind Asylum at Lambeth.

The next find was in New Scotland Yard itself — which was then in the process of being built. A workman who went into the basement to recover his tools — which he kept hidden behind some boarding in a recess, noticed a black bundle, also in the recess. When he and an assistant manager took it out into the daylight, they discovered it was a human torso with the head and arms missing. It was wrapped in a woman's black silk dress.

A further search of the basement, this time with a sniffer dog, revealed a leg and a foot belonging to the same body. The pathologist commented that the foot seemed exceptionally well-shaped, and probably did not belong to a woman of the working-class.

Two police doctors agreed that the arms already found belonged to the same body. One of them was of the opinion that the hands again showed a woman who was not used to manual labour.

The speculation in the newspapers that this dismemberment was the work of Jack the Ripper, led to a letter to the Central Newsagency — to which previous Ripper letters had been sent — in which the writer, who signed himself 'Jack the Ripper', swore solemnly that the victim found near the Thames had nothing to do with him. He went on to promise another triple murder — which never took place.

Chapter Two

Early Twentieth-Century Unsolved Murders

B y the turn of the century, new methods of forensic analysis were turning crime detection into a science. There was the discovery of fingerprints, of blood groups, and of ballistics - methods of identifying which gun had fired a particular bullet. Ballistics played a part in the conviction of a villainous con-man named Samuel Herbert Dougal, who murdered his mistress Camille Holland in 1899 — after she ordered him to leave her home — and buried her body in the garden of Moat Farm, Essex. Dougal continued to live there for the next four years, forging cheques in the name of Miss Holland and seducing servant girls. When the police finally came to enquire about Miss Holland, he fled, but was captured in London. A decomposed female corpse was found in the garden of Moat Farm. It bore no distinguishing marks, but Camille Holland's shoemaker was able to identify the initialled boots found with the body. And the testimony of firearms expert Edward J. Churchill convinced a jury that Dougal had shot Miss Holland at a range of a few inches — he tested his theory by firing bullets at the skull of a sheep, and learned that the further away from the gun, the bigger the hole it made. Dougal confessed to the murder as he stood on the scaffold.

Churchill was also to play a central role in a case that is still regarded as one of the oddest unsolved mysteries of the twentieth century: the Luard mystery.

But the Luard case seems typically British; it has the bland atmosphere of an Agatha Christie novel. Across the Atlantic, murder was usually more violent and less mysterious. The unsolved murder of Nora Fuller which occurred in San Francisco *has the dubious distinction of being one of the first recorded sex crimes of the twentieth century. And the New Orleans Axeman as the classic American murder mystery of the World War I period has something in common with London's Jack the Ripper murders of 1888.*

The Summer House Mystery

On 24 August 1908, fifty-eight-year-old Caroline Mary Luard, attractive wife of seventy-year-old Major-General Charles Edward Luard, was found shot dead in a summer-house close to the Luards' rural residence, Ightham Knoll, near Sevenoaks in Kent. The couple had left their house at 2.30 that afternoon. General Luard's destination was Godden Green golf links, three miles away, from which he wished to collect his golf clubs in preparation for a weekend visit. His wife parted from him after walking a short distance, her intention being to proceed to the "Casa", an unoccupied woodland bungalow surrounded by bracken, from which there was a pleasing view of the countryside. Returning from the links, General Luard refused a lift from a car-owning friend, the Reverend R. B. Cotton. At home by 4.30, the General entertained a Mrs Stuart to tea, expressing surprise that his wife had not returned. By early evening he went to the Casa, and found Mrs Luard prone on the verandah, two bullets in her head and four valuable rings missing from her left hand. (During the post-mortem it was established that the rings had been removed some time after the shooting.)

Police fixed the murder time: Mrs Annie Wickham, wife of a neighbour's coachman, had heard shots at 3.15, as had Daniel Kettle, a farm labourer. There was an absence of clues, although much talk of mysterious strangers seen in the vicinity – not unlikely, for hop-picking Eastenders were

Mary Sophia Money was an attractive girl who earned her own living working as a dairymaid. In September 1905, she was living at 245 Lavender Hill, Clapham, and was not known to have any men friends. On Sunday 24 September, 1905, she told another dairymaid she was going out for a little walk. She called in the nearby sweet shop at 7 o'clock and said she was going to Victoria. At 11 that night her body was found in the Merstham Tunnel, near Merstham, on the Brighton line. She had been badly disfigured by the train and had apparently been pushed or fallen out in the tunnel.

A signalman at Purley Oaks said that, as a train had passed, he had seen a couple struggling, and the man seemed to be trying to force the girl onto the seat.

No one ever discovered the name of the man Mary Money was going to meet at Victoria, or why she allowed herself to be persuaded to get on the train for Brighton. But it seems that, whoever he was, they began to argue on the way to Brighton — perhaps whether she should stay the night with him — and he pushed her out of the carriage.

Mary Money's brother, Robert Henry Money, was a dairy farmer who lived a double life. He had affairs with two sisters, and had two children by one of them, and one by the other (whom he married.) In 1912, seven years after his sister's death, he took both women to Eastbourne, shot the women and the three children, and then set fire to the house with petrol before shooting himself. One of the women succeeded in escaping.

Some writers on the mystery have suggested that Robert Money may have had something to do with the death of his sister, but no connection between the two tragedies was ever found.

in Kent at this time enjoying their annual working holiday; nor had the General's wife any enemies. At the inquest General Luard was asked about firearms he kept at Ightham Knoll, and said he had not missed any revolver. The Reverend R. B. Cotton, questioned about his own mysterious stranger, mentioned a "sandy-haired tramp" he had seen emerge from the woods about the time of the murder. A juryman was assured that no certified lunatic had a grudge against Mrs Luard. Upon the adjournment of this inquest, General Luard himself became chief suspect and received many abusive letters.

The autopsy had disclosed that Caroline Luard had been shot twice with a .32 revolver. Luard himself had owned several revolvers of this calibre, and these were sent to Churchill — who ran a gun business in the Strand — for examination. Churchill fired test bullets from each of the guns, then examined them under a microscope. The difference in the rifle marks established that none of them had fired the murder bullet.

At the second inquest Mr Thomas Durrand, manager of a Sevenoaks brewery, spoke of seeing General Luard at 3.20 near Hall Farm, a quarter-hour's walk from the Casa. Ernest King, a labourer, testified that he saw General Luard walking towards Godden Green Golf Club at 3.25, twenty minutes' walk from the Casa, and Harry Kent, steward of the golf club, said he had seen General Luard on the eighteenth green at 3.30. All three witnesses spoke of the General's composure of manner. Servants at Ightham

Knoll testified to the Luards' devotion, and General Luard himself, haggard and grief-stricken, presented a pitiful figure in the witness-box. This second inquest was adjourned, and General Luard, after putting up Ightham Knoll for sale, went to stay with his friend, Colonel Ward, MP. One morning he walked out and threw himself under a train near the local junction at West Farleigh. He had left Ward a letter saying he could not stand the strain of being under suspicion. To another friend he left a note:

> I have gone to her I loved. Goodbye. Something has snapped.
>
> > Luard

Sixty years later, in 1959, when the present writer was compiling *An Encyclopaedia of Murder*, a correspondent sent me a copy of a paper on capital punishment by C. H. Norman, who had been at one time an official shorthand writer to the Court of Criminal Appeal. In this paper — which I included as an appendix in the *Encyclopaedia* — Norman stated his conviction that the killer of Mrs Luard was the "railway murderer" John Dickman, who was convicted in 1910 of murdering a wages clerk named Nisbet on a Newcastle train, and stealing £370. Nisbet was shot in the head five times. Sir S. Rowan-Hamilton, who edited the trial of Dickman for the *Notable British Trials* series, told Norman in a letter: "All the same Dickman was justly convicted, and it may interest you to know that he was with little doubt the murderer of Mrs Luard, for he had forged a cheque she had sent him in response to an advertisement in *The Times* (I believe) asking for help; she discovered it and wrote to him and met him outside the General's and her house and her body was found there. He was absent from Newcastle those exact days . . . I have seen replicas of the cheques."

Whether this is the true solution of the Luard mystery will never be known. The only conclusive piece of evidence would have been the gun with which Caroline Luard was shot. But the two guns used to kill Nisbet were never found; and if Dickman shot Caroline Luard, he undoubtedly took the same care to dispose of the .32 revolver that he used. Even as early as 1910, murderers who used guns were becoming aware of the danger posed by firearms experts.

The Murder of Nora Fuller by a Degenerate

This, one of the first recorded sex crimes, is recounted in a typically leisurely manner by San Francisco police captain Thomas S. Duke, in his classic *Celebrated Criminal Cases of America*, published in 1910.

Eleanor Parline, better known as Nora Fuller, was born in China in 1886.

In 1890 her father was an engineer on the Steamer Tai Wo. One night he was sitting asleep in a steamer chair on the deck of the vessel while at sea. Shortly after he was seen in this position his services were required in the engine-room, but when a helper was sent after him the chair was vacant, and Parline was never seen again. A year later Mrs. Parline married a man named W. W. Fuller, in San Francisco, but seven years later she obtained a divorce.

As she had four small children, Mrs. Fuller experienced much trouble in getting along. In 1902 she lived at 1747 Fulton Street. At that time Nora, who was then fifteen years of age, decided to quit school and seek employment.

On 6 January she wrote to a theatrical agency, and after stating that she had a fairly good soprano voice, asked for employment. Two days later the following advertisement appeared in the Chronicle and Examiner:

"Wanted — Young white girl to take care of baby; good home and good wages."

At the foot of the advertisement was a note directing anyone answering, to address the communication in care of the paper the advertisement was found in. Nora Fuller answered it, and on Saturday, 11 January, she received the following postal card:

"Miss Fuller: In answer to yours in response to my advertisement, kindly call at the Popular restaurant, 55 Geary Street, and inquire for Mr. John Bennett, at 1 o'clock. If you can't come at 1, come at 6.
                                        JOHN BENNETT."

Mrs. Fuller sent Nora to rendezvous, and the girl took the postal card with her. About one hour later Mrs. Fuller's telephone rang, and her twelve-year-old son answered.

A nervous, irritable voice, which sounded something like Nora's, told him that the speaker was at the home of Mr. Bennett, at 1500 Geary Street, and her employer wanted her to go to work at once.

The boy called out the message to his mother, who instructed him to tell Nora to come home and go to work Monday. The boy repeated the message, and the person at the other end said: "All right"; but before any more could be said by the boy the receiver at the other end was hung up. Nora Fuller never came home. A few days later the distracted mother notified the police.

> In their book *Perfect Murder*, Bernard Taylor and Stephen Knight conclude that there is no evidence whatever that Mrs Luard was murdered by railway-killer Dickman. Their view is that she was killed by some casual intruder intent on burglary. They point out that the month when she was killed was the middle of the hop-picking season, when hundreds of Londoners go to Kent for a paid holiday. Some East End crook who carried a gun (gun laws were far more lax in 1908) may have been on the lookout for somewhere to burgle, and been in the summer house when Mrs Luard came. The fact that her rings were removed and a pocket (probably containing her purse) was torn off adds some support to this theory.

F. W. Krone, proprietor of the Popular restaurant, was questioned and he stated that about 5:30 o'clock on the evening of 11 January, a man who had been a patron of his place at different times during the past fifteen years, but whose name he had not up to that time heard, came to the counter and stated that he expected a young girl to inquire for John Bennett, and if she did, to send her to the table where he was seated.

The girl did not appear, and Bennett, after waiting one-half hour, became restless and walked up and down the side-walk in front of the restaurant for several moments. He then disappeared.

This man was described as being about forty years of age, five feet nine inches high, weighing about 170 pounds, wearing a brown mustache, well dressed and of refined appearance.

A waiter employed at the Popular restaurant, who frequently waited on "Bennett", stated that the much-wanted man was a great lover of porterhouse steaks, but the fact that he only ate the tenderloin part of the steak earned for him the sobriquet of "Tenderloin".

On 16 January lengthy articles were published in the papers in regard to the mysterious disappearance of the girl.

On January 8 a man giving the name of C. B. Hawkins called at Umbsen & Co.'s real estate office, and, addressing a clerk named C. S. Lahenier, inquired for particulars regarding a two-storey frame building for rent at 2211 Sutter Street. The terms were satisfactory to Hawkins, but Lahenier asked the prospective tenant for references. He replied that he could give none, as he was a stranger in the city, but as he had a prepossessing appearance the clerk let him have the key after paying one month's rent in advance. The man then signed the name "C. B. Hawkins" to a contract.

He stated that he was then stopping at the Golden West Hotel with his wife. The description of Hawkins was identical to the description of Bennett.

On the following day the real estate firm sent E. F. Bertrand, a locksmith and "handy man" in their employ, to the Sutter Street house to clean it up.

Many days after this, a collector for the firm named Fred Crawford reported that the house was still vacant — judging from outside appearances. He went to the Golden West Hotel to inquire for Hawkins, but he was not known there.

On 8 February the month's rent was up, and a collector and inspector named H. E. Dean was sent to the house.

Using a pass key he entered, but finding no furniture on the lower floor, he went upstairs, where he found the door to a back room closed. This he opened, but as the shade was down the room was in semi-darkness. He discerned a bright-colored garment on the floor, but as he seemed to know by intuition that something was wrong, he hurriedly left the building, and meeting Officer Gill requested him to accompany him back to the house. The officer entered the room, and upon raising the shade found the dead body of a young girl lying as if asleep in a bed. On the bed were two new sheets, which had never been laundered, a blanket and quilt. An old chair was the only other furniture in the house. Neither food nor dishes could be found. Nor was there any means of heating or lighting the house, as the gas was not connected.

The girl's clothing was in the bedroom, also her purse, which contained no money, but a card with the following inscription thereon:

"Mr. M. A. Severbrinik, of Port Arthur."

(It was subsequently learned that this man sailed for China on the *Peking* three hours before Nora Fuller left home on 11 January.)

On the floor was the butt of a cigar, and on the mantelpiece in the front room was an almost empty whisky bottle. There were no toilet articles in the house except one towel.

Many letters were found addressed to Mrs. C. B. Hawkins, 2211 Sutter Street. They were from furniture houses and contained either advertisements or solicitations for trade. A circular letter addressed to Mrs. Hawkins and bearing a postmark of 21 January, 11 p.m., or ten days after the disappearance of Nora Fuller, had been opened by someone and then placed in the girl's jacket, which was found in the room.

Mrs. Fuller identified the clothing as belonging to her daughter, and subsequently identified the body as the remains of Nora. No trace was ever found of the postal card Nora received from Bennett.

Dr. Charles Morgan, the city toxicologist, examined the stomach and found no traces of drugs or poisons. Save for an apple, which the deceased had evidently eaten about one or two hours before death, the stomach was empty.

There was a slight congestion of the stomach, possibly due to partaking of some alcoholic drink when the stomach was not accustomed to it. Mrs. Fuller stated that Nora ate an apple shortly before she left home on 11 January.

Dr. Bacigalupi, the autopsy surgeon, found two black marks on the throat, one on each side of the larynx, and as there was a slight congestion of the lungs, he concluded that death was due to strangulation. But the child had been otherwise assaulted and her body frightfully mutilated, evidently by a degenerate. Captain of Detectives John Seymour took charge of the case.

B. T. Schell, a salesman at J. C. Cavanaugh's furniture store, located at 848 Mission Street, stated that at 5 p.m., 9 January, a man of the same description as "Hawkins" or "Bennett," and wearing a high silk hat, called and said that he wanted to furnish a room temporarily. He purchased two second-hand pillows, a pair of blankets, a comforter and top mattress. He insisted that the goods be delivered at night or not at all. This Schell promised to do. The customer then wanted to know what assurance he had that the salesman would not substitute another mattress, and Schell suggested that he put his initials on the mattress as a means of identification. Acting on this suggestion Hawkins used a large heavy pencil and wrote the letters "C. B. H." on the mattress. After leaving word to deliver the articles that night to 2211 Sutter Street the man departed.

Lawrence C. Gillen, the delivery boy for this firm, stated that he had to work overtime in order to take the articles to the Sutter Street house that night.

When he arrived the house was in darkness. He rang the bell and a man came to the door, and from what he could see with the lights from the street lamps, he was of the same description as the man who made the purchases, and he wore a silk hat. Gillen asked him to light up so he could see, but he said, "Never mind, leave the things in the hall."

Richard Fitzgerald, a salesman employed at the Standard Furniture Company, 745 Mission Street, stated that a man of "Bennett's" description bought a bed and an old chair from him on 10 January, and that he engaged an expressman, Tom Tobin, to deliver the same to 2211 Sutter Street.

Tobin stated that this man was present when he arrived, and requested him to set up the bed in the room where it was found. This man he described as being of Bennett's appearance.

It is probable that the sheets, towel and pillow cases were purchased at Mrs. Mahoney's dry goods store, 92 Third Street, which was just around the corner from the Standard Furniture Company. These articles were carried away by the purchaser.

On the floor of the room where the girl's body was found was a small piece of the Denver Post of 9 January, upon which was a mailing label addressed to the office of the Railroad Employees' Journal, 210 Parrott Building.

When this paper arrived at the Parrott building it was given by Exchange Editor Scott to a Mr. Hurlburt, a delegate from Denver to a railroadmen's convention then in session in the assemblyroom in the Parrott building. After glancing at it he threw it on a large table, and some other delegate picked it up and took it to Dennett's restaurant, where he left it on the dining table. The steward of the restaurant, Mr. Helbish, picked it up, and after taking it to the counter began to read it, believing it was the San Francisco Post. He laid it down, and Miss Drysdale, the cashier, glanced over it. She laid it down, and how it got to 2211 Sutter Street remains a mystery.

A seventeen-year-old girl named Madge Graham met Nora Fuller in June, 1901, and they became very friendly. Madge boarded at Nora's house for a while until her guardian, Attorney Edward Stearns, requested her to move away, because a lawyer named Hugh Grant was a frequent visitor at the Fuller home.

She claimed that Nora Fuller frequently spoke to her of having a friend named Bennett, also she believed that the advertisement was a trick concocted by Nora and "Bennett" to deceive Mrs. Fuller.

She furthermore stated that Nora often telephoned to some man, and that one day Nora requested her to tell Mrs. Fuller that she and Nora were going to the theater that night. Madge did as requested, but stated that instead of going with her, Nora went with some man. It was also claimed that someone gave Nora complimentary press tickets to the theaters.

A. Menke, who conducted a grocery at Golden Gate and Central Avenues, stated that Nora Fuller frequently used his telephone to call up someone at a hotel, although she had a telephone in her own home a few blocks away.

Theodore Kytka, the handwriting expert, made an examination of the original slips filled out by "Bennett" for his advertisement for a young girl, and also the signature of "C. B. Hawkins" to the contract when they rented the house, and found both were written by the same person.

On 19 February the Coroner's jury rendered the following verdict:

"That the said Nora Fuller, aged fifteen, nativity China, residence 1747 Fulton Street, came to her death at 2211 Sutter Street in the City and County of San Francisco, through asphyxiation by strangling on a day subsequent to 11 January and before 4 February, 1902, at the hands of parties unknown. Furthermore we believe that she died within twenty-four hours after 12 m., 11 January. In view of the heinousness of the crime, we recommend that the Governor offer a reward of $5,000 for the discovery and apprehension of the criminal.

"ACHILLE ROSS, Foreman."

Believing that the person who committed this crime might have changed his address and sent a written notification to that effect to the postal authorities, Theodore Kytka examined 32,000 notifications of changes of address. Of this number he found three signatures that bore considerable resemblance to the Bennett—Hawkins style of penmanship, and one of these three was almost identically the same.

This proved to be the signature of a man in Kansas City, Mo., and Captain Seymour went east to make a personal investigation. It was found, however, that the man had nothing to do with the crime.

On 16 January, five days after the disappearance of Nora Fuller, but three weeks before her fate was known, the papers of San Francisco gave considerable space to the mysterious case. Two days later a gentleman connected with a local paper notified the police department that a clerk in their employ named Charles B. Hadley had disappeared. It was afterward said that he was short in his accounts with his employers.

Detective Charles Cody was detailed to locate the man, and he found that he had lived at 647 Ellis Street with a girl born and raised in San Francisco, who had assumed the name of Ollie Blasier, because of her infatuation for a notorious character known as "Kid" Blasier.

No trace of Hadley was found. Finally the body of Nora Fuller was discovered, and photographs of the signature of "C. B. Hawkins" on the contract with Umbsen & Co., and the "C. B. H." on the mattress, were published in all the papers.

The Blasier woman had a photograph of Hadley in her room, upon the back of which he had written his name, "C. B. Hadley." Seeing the great similarity in the handwriting she delivered this to Detective Cody, who in turn delivered it to Theodore Kytka for investigation.

Kytka determined at once that the person who wrote "C. B. Hadley" on the photograph also wrote "C. B. H." on the mattress, and "C. B. Hawkins" on the contract.

While Hadley had the same general physique as "Hawkins," it was known that he was always clean shaven. Miss Blasier stated, however, that she had seen Hadley wear a false brown mustache about the house, and it was subsequently learned that he purchased one at a Japanese store on Larkin Street.

In addition to this, Chief of Police Langley, of Victoria, B.C., made an affidavit to the effect that a Mr. Marsden, a storekeeper in Victoria, B.C., had stated that he had been a companion of Hadley's, and that while out on a "lark" he had seen Hadley wear a false mustache. Miss Blasier made a further statement as follows:

"I now recall that after the disappearance of Nora Fuller, Hadley made a practice of getting up early in the morning and taking the morning paper to the toilet to read.

"On the day of his final disappearance he followed this practice, and after he left the house I found the morning paper in the toilet, and I noticed a long article about the disappearance of Nora Fuller. It was evident that his mind was greatly disturbed on this morning.

"The next day I was making up my laundry, and at the very bottom of the pile of soiled clothing I found some of his garments which had blood on them. I burned them and also his plug hat.

"It is well known that Hadley is partial to porterhouse steaks and that he eats only the tenderloin.

"On the evening of 16 January, Hadley telephoned to me that he would not be home. I confess that I suspect he committed this murder."

Theodore Kytka obtained Hadley's photograph and altered it by giving him the appearance of wearing a mustache and plug hat. This was shown to different persons who had dealings with "Hawkins," with the following results:

Tobin, the expressman, said it looked very much like him; Lahenier, the real estate man, said it bore a marked resemblance. Ray Zertanna, who had seen Nora in the park with a man, stated that the picture was a good likeness of this man. Schell, who suggested that "Hawkins" place his initials on the mattress, said it was an exact likeness of Hawkins.

Fred Krone, the restaurant man, who had the conversation with "Bennett" on the evening Nora left home, said it was not a likeness of Bennett.

Hadley left his money in a certain bank in the city, where it remains even now.

An investigation was then made as to his past, and it developed that he was an habitue of the tenderloin district, and that he was on the road to degeneracy. His true name was Charlie Start, and his respected mother resided in Chicago.

On 6 May, 1889, Superintendent of Police Brackett, of Minneapolis, issued a circular letter offering $100 reward for the arrest of Charles Start for embezzlement.

About two years before the murder of Nora Fuller, Hadley enticed a fifteen-year-old girl into a room and outraged her. He then purchased diamonds and jewelry from a certain large jewelry store in San Francisco and gave them to the girl, who is now a respectable married woman residing in the neighborhood of San Francisco.

The country was flooded with circulars accusing Hadley of this murder and calling for his apprehension, but he was never located.

Many believe that he committed suicide.

The Willie Starchfield Case

On 8 January, 1914, a fifteen-year-old errand boy entered a train compartment of the North London Railway Company at Mildmay Park at about four in the afternoon. He noticed a small hand sticking out from beneath the seat, but was too frightened to examine it. At Dalston he tried to attract the attention of a porter, but failed. At the next station,

Haggerston, he fled from the train, but then went and told the station master. The train was halted at the next station, and the body of the five-year-old boy was found under the seat.

Willie Starchfield's mother and father were separated. His father, John Starchfield, sold newspapers in Tottenham Court Road. The boy lived with his mother, Agnes in Hampstead Road. That day, he'd been sent on an errand at 12.50, but failed to return.

Doctor Bernard Spilsbury calculated that death had taken place some time between 2 and 3 o'clock. The body had then been pushed under the seat, and apparently the train had gone back and forth several times between Chalk Farm Station and Broad Street.

The next day, a search of the railway line uncovered a piece of cord not far from Shoreditch Station. It looked as if it had been dropped from a window of a passing train, and seemed to fit the groove around Willie Starchfield's throat.

Suspicion began to fall on the father, John Starchfield. A Mrs Wood said that she was in Kentish Town around 1 o'clock when she saw a man leading a little boy by the hand. The boy was eating a piece of currant cake and she remembered his golden curls. A commercial traveller named White saw the same little boy with the man at Camden Town Station around 2 o'clock.

At the inquest, both the witnesses picked out John Starchfield as the man they had seen. Starchfield was arrested and charged with murder.

The problem was, why should Starchfield want to kill his own son? It seemed unlikely that he would do this simply to spite his wife. Chief Inspector William Gough theorised that Starchfield had intended to try to persuade the boy to leave his mother to live with him, had met him in the street, and then persuaded him to go for a train ride. On the train, Starchfield had probably tried to persuade his son to leave his mother and come and live with him. If Willie refused, despite all his father's arguments, Starchfield may have lost his temper and hit the boy. Then, perhaps in a fit of rage, or to stifle his cries, he pulled a piece of cord out of his pocket — the cord used to tie up bundles of newspapers — and strangled him. Spilsbury said that the child was in a condition of *status lymphaticus*, which meant that he might easily die if he received a severe shock.

Still another witness who knew Starchfield well, said that he saw Starchfield leading Willie by the hand around 2 o'clock that day.

It looked an open and shut case, but when it came into court on 9 March, 1914, Gough realised that his evidence was less strong than he had hoped. A witness who knew Starchfield tried to commit suicide before he could appear in court. Mrs Wood admitted that she had seen Starchfield's photograph in a newspaper before she identified him, and was confused about the kind of hat he was wearing when she saw him. The judge criticised the coroner for inefficiency, and told the jury to return a verdict of Not Guilty.

Starchfield died two years later, still strongly protesting his innocence, and insisting that the crime had been committed by somebody as an act of revenge. In 1912 he had helped arrest an armed madman who had been firing at random in the bar of a hotel. Starchfield was wounded in the struggle, and awarded one pound a week by the Carnegie Heroes' Fund. Starchfield thought that it was some friend of the madman, Stephen Titus, who had murdered his son. Chief Inspector Gough remained convinced that Starchfield was the killer.

The New Orleans Axeman

On the morning of 24 May 1918, an Italian cobbler named Jake Maggio was awakened by a groaning sound coming from the next room, where his brother Joe slept with his wife. As he entered the room, he saw a woman lying on the floor, her head almost severed from her body; Joe lay in bed groaning. Nearby lay a bloodstained axe and a cut-throat razor, which had been used to slash Joe's throat. He died soon after.

By the time the police arrived, Jake and his second brother Andrew had found how the intruder entered — through a panel chiselled out of the back door. Jake and Andrew were arrested as suspects, but soon released.

On the pavement two streets away someone had chalked on the pavement: "Mrs Maggio is going to sit up tonight, just like Mrs Toney". It reminded the police that seven years earlier there had been four axe murders of Italian grocers, including a Mrs Tony Schiambra. They had been attributed to the criminal organization "the Black Hand", which was rife in New Orleans.

Five weeks after the Maggio killings, a bread delivery man found a back door with a panel chiselled out. When he knocked the door was opened by a man covered in blood. He was a Pole named Besumer, and inside lay a woman who was known as his wife. She was still alive, and told of being struck by a big white man wielding a hatchet. She died later, and Besumer was charged with her murder. But that night the axeman struck again — a young married man, Edward Schneider, returned home to find his pregnant wife lying in bed covered in blood. Rushed to hospital, she survived, and gave birth a week later. The attacker seemed to have entered by an open window.

Five days later, a barber named Romano became the next victim. His niece heard noises in his bedroom, and went in to find him being attacked by a big man wearing a black slouch hat. As she screamed the man "vanished as if he had wings". A panel had been chipped out of the door.

New Orleans was in a panic reminiscent of that which had swept London in the days of Jack the Ripper. There were several false alarms, and one man found an axe and chisel outside his back door. On 30 August 1918 a man named Nick Asunto heard a noise, and went to investigate; he saw a heavily-built man with an axe, who fled as he shouted. All New Orleans began taking elaborate precautions against the Axeman.

For the time being, the attacks ceased, and the ending of the war in 1918 gave people other things to think about. But in March 1919, a grocer named Jordano heard screams from a house across the street, and found another grocer, Charles Cortimiglia, unconscious on the floor, while his wife — a dead baby in her arms — sat on the floor with blood streaming from her head. She said she had awakened to see a man attacking her husband with an axe, and when she snatched up her baby, he killed the child with a blow, then struck her . . . The door panel had been chiselled out. Yet when Mrs Cortimiglia began to recover, she accused Jordano, the man who had found her, of being the killer, and although her husband (now also recovering) insisted that this was untrue, Jordano and his son were arrested.

Three days after the attack, the local newspaper received a letter signed "The Axeman", datelined "From Hell" (as in the case of a Jack the Ripper letter), and declaring that he would be coming to New Orleans next Tuesday at 12.15, but would spare any house playing jazz music. The following Tuesday, the streets of New Orleans rocked with jazz, and the Axeman failed to appear . . . Someone even wrote a "Mysterious Axeman Jazz".

Besumer, who had been in custody since his arrest, was tried and acquitted. But the Jordanos, to everyone's amazement, were found guilty, although Charles Cortimiglia repeated that they were innocent.

And the attacks went on — although there was to be only one further death. On 10 August 1919, a grocer named Steve Boca woke to find a shadowy figure holding an axe beside the bed. When he woke again, he was bleeding from a skull wound. He managed to stagger down to the home of a friend, Frank Genusa, and the frantic police arrested Genusa — then shamefacedly released him.

On 2 September, a druggist named Carlson heard scratching noises from the back door, and fired his revolver through the panel. The intruder fled, leaving behind a chisel. The next day, neighbours found nineteen-year-old Sarah Lauman unconscious; she had been attacked with an axe and three teeth knocked out. She could remember nothing when she recovered.

The last attack was on a grocer named Mike Pepitone. His wife — in a separate bedroom — heard sounds of a struggle, and entered his room in time to see a man vanishing. Her husband had been killed with an axe blow so violent that it splattered blood up the wall. Again, a chiselled door panel revealed how the axeman had gained entry.

Then the murders ceased. The Jordanos were finally released when Mrs Cortimiglia confessed that she had lied because she hated them. Now, she said, her husband had left her, and she had smallpox — Saint Joseph had appeared to her and told her to confess. The Jordanos were released.

But Mrs Pepitone, widow of the last victim, was to enter the story again. On 7 December 1920, in Los Angeles, she had shot and killed a man named Joseph Mumfre, from New Orleans, in the street. She claimed he was the Axeman. She was sentenced to ten years in prison, but released after three.

Was Mumfre the Axeman? He could well have been. He had been released from prison just before the 1911 murders, then sent back for the next seven years. Released again just before the first of the 1918 murders, he had been back in prison during the "lull" between August 1918 and March 1919, when they began again. He left New Orleans shortly after the murder of Mike Pepitone.

What was his motive? Almost certainly, he was a sadist who wanted to attack women, not men. Joe Maggio was left alive; his wife was killed. Besumer was only knocked unconscious; his attractive wife died of her injuries. Many of the later victims were women, and it seems likely that he attacked the men when in search of women victims.

Why Italian grocers? In fact, many of the victims were not Italians. *But all kept small shops*. And a small shop is a place where an attractive wife can be seen serving behind the counter. Mrs Pepitone never revealed how she tracked down Mumfre, but it seems likely that he was a customer, and she recognized him and followed his trail to Los Angeles.

The Murder of Evelyn Foster

The murder of Evelyn Foster at Otterburn, Northumberland, remains unsolved.

Evelyn Foster, 27, was the daughter of a garage proprietor of Otterburn, and often active as a hire-car driver.

On a freezing evening in early January 1931, a bus driving over the desolate moors between Otterburn and Newcastle passed a car that was smouldering about 70 yards from the road. The driver went to investigate, and on the far side of the car, found Evelyn Foster, all her clothes burned off, in a state of severe pain. The girl was taken to her home, and soon afterwards she died. But in the meantime, she had succeeded in telling her story.

That afternoon, in a village called Ellishaw, a strange man told her that he wanted to get to Ponteland to catch a bus to Newcastle, and at 7.30 that evening, she picked him up near Ellishaw and drove as far as a place called Belsay. There, the man has made some kind of sexual advances to her, and when she refused, hit her in the eye so hard that she lost consciousness. The man then drove her in the car to a place called Wolf's Neck where it was found and drove out on to the moors. There, it seems, he dowsed the car in petrol, then set it alight. She opened the door and fell out onto the grass. She said that she saw the man go back to the road, saw another car stop for him, and heard a conversation before the other car drove away.

At the inquest, some puzzling contradictions arose. Her face was not only unburned, but unmarked — there was no sign of a black eye or a bruise due to being hit violently enough to knock her unconscious. Evelyn Foster had also told her mother that she had been 'sexually interfered with'. Yet again, there was no evidence of attempted sexual assault.

In spite of this, the jury brought a verdict of murder by person or persons unknown.

One suggestion that has been made is that Evelyn Foster accidentally set fire to herself in the process of burning the car in the course of an intended criminal fraud. There *were* two insurance policies, amounting to more than £1,100. But it seemed that Evelyn Foster was not in any financial trouble — she had £1,400 in the bank.

The idea that she died accidentally is also contradicted by the fact that she claimed her passenger had told her that he'd been picked up at Jedburgh by three Scottish motorists and had had tea with them. The police succeeded in locating three motorists, but they denied giving a lift to anyone that day. The killer — whom Evelyn Foster described as a small man wearing a bowler hat and a dark coat, and speaking like a gentleman, must have seen the three Scottish motorists for they actually existed. This means that he himself must have existed.

And what about the car that stopped and picked up the killer? Would the driver not be curious about the car burning a few yards away? Or did the killer claim that he had had an accident that had caused his car to burst into flame? In that case, why did not the driver of the other car come forward when the case was publicised?

Evelyn Foster's money was untouched. So the motive was not robbery. But if it was sexual assault, why did he not carry out his intention while she was unconscious? Why did he set fire to the car?

Evelyn Foster usually took a male garage employee with her when she acted as a hire-car driver. Why did she not do so on this occasion, although her sister asked her to? Did she know the man who attacked her? All these questions remain unanswered.

Trunk Murders

On 17 June, 1934, the Brighton cloakroom attendants noticed an unpleasant smell in the office. The police traced it to a cheap-looking trunk, and it was opened in the police station. It was found to contain the torso of a woman wrapped in brown paper, and tied with window cord. A word written on the paper had been half obliterated by a bloodstain, but its second half read 'ford'. Cloakrooms all over the country were searched for the rest of the body, and the result was that a pair of legs was found in a suitcase at Kings Cross.

The trunk and the suitcase had both been deposited on Derby Day 6 June, between 6 and 7 in the evening; the person responsible had judged correctly that the cloakroom attendants would be too busy to remember customers. All the attendant could recollect was that the trunk had been left by a man.

Sir Bernard Spilsbury verified that the legs and trunk belonged to the same body, a woman in her mid-20s, and had been five months pregnant. The hairs on her legs were bleached with sunbathing and some light-brown hairs on the body suggested a permanent wave — which indicated that she belonged to a reasonable income group. The brown paper in which the torso was wrapped had been soaked in olive oil — which might have suggested a restaurateur or some fairly well-to-do household. Yet although the crime was widely publicised, and over 700 missing women were traced, the identity of the victim remained a mystery. The maker of the trunk was found, in Leyton, but he had no record of what shop it had gone to. But one of his employees proved to have written the word 'ford' on the paper. Five thousand pre-natal cases were traced and eliminated. At last, the trunk was traced to a big shop in Brighton, and it looked as if all this effort was at last yielding some results, but once again, clues simply ran out. The 'Brighton Trunk Murderer' had proved that it *was* possible to commit a perfect crime.

At the same time as the unsolved Brighton trunk murder, another trunk murder in Brighton made the police feel that they may have arrested the culprit.

On 14 June, 1934, a petty crook called Tony Mancini was picked up by the police, and questioned about the Brighton trunk murder. He was released, but fled to London. His landlady, concerned about the smell coming from the trunk he had left in his room in Kemp Street, Brighton, opened it and saw that it contained a decaying female corpse. Mancini was arrested while hitch-hiking, and brought back to Brighton.

The dead woman proved to be forty-two-year-old Violette Kaye, an ex-chorus girl who had turned to prostitution. Mancini had moved in with Violette, and had been supported by her. But she was a woman of a highly jealous disposition, and one day started a furious argument in the café where Mancini worked — the cause being a waitress with whom Mancini was flirting.

Violette had died from a blow on the head, and Sir Bernard Spilsbury was forced to admit in court that it could have been caused by a fall down the steps to the basement where she lived — particularly if she was drunk at the time. Mancini claimed that he had come home from work and found her lying dead, and then lost his nerve, knowing that he had a long police record.

Mancini was acquitted. But in 1976, 42 years later, he confessed to a Sunday newspaper that he had, in fact, killed Violette Kaye in the course of a quarrel.

Chapter Three

American Mysteries

I t would be a mistake to assume that America has had no classic unsolved murders in the Agatha Christie tradition. In fact, the famous Elwell case has been described as one of the classic murder mysteries of the century.

Another remarkable unsolved mystery has found a place in most books on the "Jazz Age"; in fact, the strange death of Starr Faithfull has become one of the recurring symbols of the Prohibition era. Violence, as once remarked by the American senator H. Rap Brown, is as American as cherry pie and this comment is certainly exemplified by some of America's most famous murder mysteries, such as the Axeman of New Orleans (see page 46) and the Evangelista murders. But perhaps the nearest equivalent to London's Jack the Ripper murders is the strange case of Cleveland's "Mad Butcher", where the bodies were violently mutilated by decapitation.

The Murder of Joseph Elwell

J oseph Bowne Elwell was found dead by his housekeeper Marie Larsen at 8.25 on the morning of 11 June 1920. He was slumped in an expensive upholstered chair in his living room with a bullet hole in the centre of his forehead, about two inches above the bridge of his nose. Blood flowed down his face and stained an open letter on his knee. Where the bullet had left the back of his head it had blown a roughly cross-shaped hole measuring nine inches across. Much of the contents of his skull were sprayed against the wall behind or lying precariously on his shoulders. Despite the huge loss of brain tissue, Elwell was still alive; his eyelids flickered spasmodically as Mrs Larsen watched.

Exactly what happened next, the details of how he reached hospital and died at approximately 10 a.m., is a matter of claim and counter-claim. The reason that many people have differing accounts, and indeed the reason that anyone bothered to find them out, was that Joseph Elwell was a very well-known man in 1920. He frequented the same expensive New York clubs as Scott and Zelda Fitzgerald, relishing being part of that dazzling social set. Some people believe that Fitzgerald's Jay Gatsby was in part based upon Joseph Elwell.

Yet he was born to relatively poor parents. From an early age Joseph showed an incredible skill in bridge, indeed in all card games where skill was an element. He joined the Brooklyn's Irving Republican Club in order to sharpen his talent for bridge with many different partners. Soon he gained such a reputation that he began giving bridge lessons to the daughters of wealthy families. He was not a bridge teacher as such; he managed to give an impression that each paid assignment he received was taken on "as a special favour". He married a plump and reasonably well-off young lady named Helen Hanford, gaining in the process a skilled business manager. He was approached by a publisher to add to the then growing avalanche of bridge text books. His was easily the most successful. It was in fact written by Helen, using example hands and notes jotted down by the Great Man. Advanced manuals and commentaries upon tournament bridge hands followed, each selling very well.

Bridge was not Elwell's only pre-occupation at this time. Throughout his life, Elwell's need to sleep with many women was enormous. Soon after his marriage he began failing to come home. The situation became more extreme when Helen had a child. Soon he began ringing if he *would* be home for dinner. Helen was not entirely the mistreated little woman however — from the outraged and jealous letters that Elwell would fire off occasionally to his wife's male acquaintances, it would seem that she managed to adapt to the situation.

The Elwells' public affairs were in contrast, rosy. Joseph became bridge tutor to the Vanderbilt family, renowned multi-millionaires. He was a close friend of Walter Lewisohn, the millionaire New York socialite. He even gave bridge lessons to King Edward VII.

His relationship with his wife inevitably grew distant however, with Joseph permanently on the look-out for any grounds for divorce and putting a great deal of his earnings into his parents' names in order to avoid having to pay it to Helen in alimony. When they eventually separated Helen got a meagre payment, and that only on the condition that she renounced any claim to money Joseph was making on real estate deals.

Indeed, as Joseph's fortune increased so the range of his business dealings widened. He invested in race horses and Palm Beach luxury property, making money every time. He lost the investments he made in Tsarist Russia in 1917 with the Revolution, and responded by joining and sponsoring the American Protective League, a group whose espoused aim was to root out spies, but who in fact just harassed anyone living in America who was not American.

His liaisons with many women continued, made more convenient by the fact that all the servants at his West Seventieth Street apartment lived off premises. All seemed to be ideal for Joseph Bowne Elwell until someone shot him between 7.25 and 8.35 a.m. that hot June morning.

It is possible to be this exact with respect to the time of the shooting due to a strange circumstance. At 6.30 that morning Jost Otten, Elwell's milkman, delivered a pint of milk and some cream. In order to place them against Elwell's door it was necessary to open the large double doors leading to the small hall of the apartment building. This presented no problem, as they were unlocked. Likewise the postman has no difficulty getting to Elwell's postbox on the internal door at 7.25 a.m. However, when Marie Larsen arrives at 8.35 a.m. the double doors are locked. It is clear that Elwell was alive to receive his post — one of the letters was open on his knee. This leads to the conclusion that the killer had a key. All the locks on the apartment had been changed recently due to a burglary attempt — the killer acquired a key soon before the murder. The likelihood seems to be that Elwell knew his killer.

Further evidence for this is presented by what he was *not* wearing when found. Nearly everyone who knew Elwell thought he had even white teeth and attractive shiny hair. In fact he was close to completely bald, and with only three teeth in his head. His expensive wig and tailored dentures remained upstairs in his bedroom. It is unlikely he would have entertained any of his lady friends without them.

The events of the preceding evening are reasonably clear. Elwell was out on the town with Walter Lewisohn and some friends, including Viola Kraus, Lewisohn's sister-in-law, allegedly one of Elwell's mistresses. These friends left Elwell to find his own way home when he declined a taxi ride with them. This was the last certain sighting of him before Marie Larsen found him the next morning.

The word "certain" is used advisedly, as Elwell's notoriety, coupled with the detective fiction style of his death, led to a hurricane of conflicting stories regarding virtually every aspect of the known facts. As mentioned above, even the manner of his transferral to hospital is hotly debated. The newspapers tried to implicate all Elwell's friends in turn through snide innuendo, while also speculating about Elwell's ties to bootlegging and spying. So many people were intrigued by the case, and so many people took it upon themselves to investigate it that it became clear that the killer's total evasion of justice can be attributed almost entirely to too much speculation and almost no real investigation.

To present the facts without a gloss of idle rumination is thus made quite difficult. The objective details of the crime scene are among the few facts undisputed . . .

In the room where Elwell was discovered two cigarette butts were found. One of them was on the table next to Elwell's chair — a cigarette made especially to order. It had been left to burn completely. It had been lit at the wrong end i.e. the end with the manufacturers logo impressed into the paper. The other cigarette was of an over-the-counter variety. The police felt this to be such a vital clue that they refused to divulge the actual make. This cigarette had been extinguished on the mantelpiece and still showed signs of saliva on the end when Marie Larsen discovered it. For the saliva to remain partially unevaporated in the 70°F heat meant that the smoker must have drooled a great deal. In his book *The Slaying of Joseph Bowne Elwell* Jonathan Goodman asserts that the second butt was in fact left by an investigating officer, explaining their reticence to elucidate on its origins.

Upstairs the police found a great deal of lingerie in the spare bedroom. Although the newspapers got a lot of mileage out of this discovery, it seems in retrospect to be quite unimportant.

The autopsy showed that the bullet entered Elwell's forehead at an upwards angle — perhaps meaning that it was fired from the hip. Another, more melodramatic interpretation of this fact has Elwell's head bent slightly back to look into the eyes of his killer. Around the entrance wound were many small gunpowder marks — as distinct from gunpowder burns. This meant that the shot must have been fired from between three feet and five inches from Elwell's head. Any closer and Elwell's face would have been burnt by powder from the gun's barrel. This fact tends to make suicide unlikely, as few suicides shoot themselves at a distance, thus risking a painful but not fatal winging shot. The lack of the weapon tends to further invalidate suicide as an explanation.

Those are the main details — Elwell was shot within the time space of one cigarette from a point lower than his seated head and from less than three feet away. Inevitably however these facts are not enough, the imagination demands some violent and passionate motive. Passion is of course the most proffered explanation, a wronged woman, or a brother or father. Some theories go further — linking this possible motive to possible murderers. For instance Viola Kraus, Walter Lewisohn's sister-in-law and supposed lover of Elwell, met her divorced husband the night before the murders. In fact, the divorce had only just gone through that day. Viola was dancing with Elwell. Did her husband see red and kill Elwell the next morning?

Another theory has Viola herself as killer. Elwell had been belatedly discussing divorce with Helen in the weeks leading up to his death. Did Viola take this as a tacit sign that he wished to marry her when their joint divorces cleared? Did she, when she found he simply wanted more freedom to see many other women, kill him in a fit of jilted rage?

Jonathan Goodman, in *The Slaying of Joseph Bowne Elwell*, puts forward a masterfully imagined theory. Based upon the fact that Walter Lewisohn went mad two years after Elwell's killing, some say for love of a dancer Leonora Hughes, Goodman argues that Lewisohn saw Elwell's (alleged) rejection of Viola as positive proof that he was after Ms Hughes. In order to avoid this situation Lewisohn has Elwell killed by a friend — the owner of the building that Elwell leased. This neatly explains the key problem as the owner would have up-to-date keys for his own building. The theory is supported by the fact that the alleged killer received a sinecure in Lewisohn's establishment after the killing.

Most intriguing of all however is a small point that Goodman raises merely in passing. Marie Larsen was a strict Swedish Lutheran. In her opinion all suicides went to hell. Is it not possible that she removed the gun from the scene in order to save Elwell's loved ones the terrible conclusion that Joseph was in the fire for eternity?

Admittedly all these theories are at best unprovable. It is only natural that many explanations have been presented for a set of circumstances that are, at the end of the day, insoluble.

The Shooting of Father Hubert

On a freezing February evening in 1924, Father Hubert Dahme was shot down on the main street of Bridgeport, Connecticut and died instantly. Passers-by saw a dark figure running into an alley-way. Two weeks later, a hitch-hiker was questioned in nearby Norwalk and when a search of his pockets revealed a point 32 revolver — the calibre that had killed the priest — the man — an alcoholic ex-soldier named Harold Israel, was taken in for questioning. Under brutal police questioning, he broke down and confessed that he had murdered the priest in a fit of anger and despair.

The young States Attorney named Homer Cummings felt that he had a watertight case. A girl working behind the counter in the hamburger bar where Israel had taken his meals, stated that she had seen him walk past the window at about the time of the murder, and had waved to him. So by this time — although Israel had now retracted his confession — there seemed no doubt that the police had the killer.

Yet Cummings was unhappy. Something struck him as oddly wrong. Israel said he was starving, yet possessed a revolver that could be sold for the price of many meals.

Unsolved Crimes

When he questioned Israel, and learned that he had been questioned for many hours under blinding lights, he became even more unhappy. Israel's alibi is that he had been in the cinema, yet he could remember virtually nothing of the plot of the film. Cummings tried asking a number of other people who had seen the same film — and they were equally vague about the plot.

Back at the scene of the murder, choosing a bleak evening at about 8 o'clock, his assistants re-enacted the crime. The nearest street lamp was fifty yeards away, and at that distance, the 'murderer' was just a blurred figure. Next they went into the hamburger joint to talk to the waitress. The first thing Cummings noticed was that the window was covered with a layer of condensation — inevitable on a cold evening. He asked the girl to identify his assistants as they walked past — she was completely unable to see them. Cummings himself then walked up and down outside — the girl waved at two strangers but failed to identify Cummings. When he learned that she had applied for a reward, Cummings drew his own conclusions.

In court on 27 May, 1924, Cummings announced to an astonished court that he was dropping the case. The accused man burst into tears — and his subsequent history demonstrated that his brush with death had jarred him out of his alcoholism — he married happily and became a prosperous timber merchant.

Cummings' decision not to prosecute, far from damaging his career, made him something of a celebrity, and he later became Roosevelt's youngest ever Attorney General.

But the mystery of who *did* kill Father Dahme is still unsolved.

The Starr Faithfull Case

In the early morning sunshine of 8 June 1931, a beach-comber strolling along the sands at Long Beach, on the south shore of Long Island, found the body of a pretty girl. He dragged it clear of the tideline and summoned the police. They quickly identified the girl as Starr Faithfull, the twenty-five-year-old stepdaughter of Stanley Faithfull, a retired manufacturing chemist of Greenwich Village. He had reported Starr missing two days earlier.

An autopsy revealed that the girl had died by drowning about forty-eight hours earlier, and had eaten a large meal not long before she died. There was no alcohol in her system, but traces of the drug veronal. She was clad only in an expensive silk dress, and traces of sand in her lungs indicated that she had been alive as she lay in the water. There were fingertip-shaped bruises on her upper arms, and indications of rape. All this suggested that Starr had been murdered by whoever had shaken her by the arms: that he had raped her — perhaps on the beach — and then held her head under the water. On the other hand, she may have consented to intercourse in a drugged trance, then collapsed by the edge of the sea and drowned as the tide came in.

Starr was undoubtedly beautiful, and the fact that she was an heiress and the product of a Boston finishing school led the press to devote much breathless attention to the case. As reporters looked into her background, it became still more interesting. Far from being a prim young lady who had had the misfortune to be assaulted, it transpired that Starr had been sexually experienced for more than half of her brief life. At the age of eleven, it seemed, she had been seduced by a middle-aged Boston business man who was the father of schoolfriends; he had drugged her with ether and raped her. This information came from her stepfather, Stanley Faithfull, whom Starr's mother had married some ten years earlier. This relationship had continued down the years.

It also seemed that Starr had been feverishly in love with an English ship's surgeon, Dr George Jameson-Carr, who did not return her feelings. On 29 May, a week before her death, Starr had been attempting to force her drunken attentions on Dr Jameson-Carr, aboard the *Franconia*. He had persuaded her to leave, but she had hidden among the passengers; when found later, she had to be transferred to a tug and taken ashore.

It emerged that Starr had fairly serious mental problems, and had been under psychiatric treatment for years. She was not normally a heavy drinker, but was inclined to get drunk at parties. She had been on two trips to England, where she had mixed with the "bright young things", and she longed to return to Europe; unfortunately, her stepfather was not wealthy — although comfortably-off — and there was no prospect of another trip in the immediate future. So Starr spent a great deal of time hanging around the New York docks, often going aboard liners for farewell parties — which is how she became acquainted with Dr Jameson-Carr. To try to prevent her drinking bootleg gin made of raw alcohol, her stepfather used to pack her a flask of Martini.

Was it possible that Starr had gone aboard a liner and then jumped over the side when it was off Long Island? Otherwise, it was difficult to explain what she was doing on Long Island, twenty miles or so from home. Or had she been pushed overboard? If so, was it by the rapist?

A second autopsy dampened these speculations when the doctor who performed it announced that, in his opinion, she had not been raped, but had submitted voluntarily to sexual intercourse. The missing underclothes certainly suggested that she had been naked at some point.

Starr's diaries increased the lurid speculation, for they revealed that she had had many lovers, one of whom was someone called A.J.P. She seemed to be fond of him but also

The first "Locked Room Mystery" was Poe's "*Murder in the Rue Morgue*". The first locked room novel seems to have been John Ratcliffe's *Nena Sahib*. This inspired a real murder. In 1881, the wife and five children of a Berlin carter named Fritz Conrad were found hanging from hooks in a locked room. It looked as if Frau Conrad, depressed by poverty, had killed her children and committed suicide. Police Commissioner Hollman was suspicious, and when he found out that Conrad was infatuated with a young girl student, he searched the apartment for love letters. He found none, but came upon a copy of *Nena Sahib* and read Ratcliffe's account of a "perfect murder", in which the killer drilled a tiny hole in the door, passed a thread through it, and used this to draw the bolt after the murder; he then sealed up the hole with wax. Hollman examined Conrad's door, and found a similar hole, filled in with sealing wax, to which threads of horsehair still adhered. Confronted with this evidence, Conrad confessed to murdering his wife and children, and was sentenced to death.

afraid of him. One entry read: "Spent night A.J.P. Providence. Oh Horror, Horror, Horror!!!" The indications were that, for all her craving for affection, Starr was not overly fond of the physical side of sex. This seemed to be confirmed by a new item of scandal unearthed by the investigators. A year before her death, a policeman had burst into a room of a New York hotel where a girl had been screaming. He found Starr naked and bruised, while a furious young man, dressed only in his undershirt, was glaring at her. She was drunk, and there was half a bottle of gin on the table. The man identified himself as an ex-soldier named Joseph Collins, produced his discharge papers, and was allowed to go. Starr, who was very drunk, was taken to the Bellevue Hospital suffering from "acute alcoholism" and "contusions to face, jaw and upper lip". The implication seemed to be that she had taken Collins to the room for sex, then changed her mind, and the frustrated man had attacked her.

Her mental problems obviously stemmed from her early seduction by the Boston business man. Reporters soon unearthed the fact that, as a child, Starr and her sister Tucker had played with the children of Andrew J. Peters, former Congressman and Mayor of Boston, who was a distant relative of Mrs Faithfull. This could obviously be the "A.J.P." of her diary. If Peters *was* her seducer, he had certainly paid for it, for the investigation revealed that Mrs Faithfull had signed a document aquitting someone of all responsibility for damage done to Starr, in exchange for a large sum of money, probably $80,000. (Stanley Faithfull alleged it was $20,000, but his lawyer indicated that the sum was much greater.)

The story was kept alive by a new sensation at the crematorium. The cremation of the body was interrupted by officials from the District Attorney's office, who announced that it could not go ahead until there was a third inquest. After this inquest, District Attorney Elvin Edwards announced that he knew the identity of the two men who killed Starr Faithfull by holding her head underwater, and that he would be making an arrest within thirty-six hours. When the arrest failed to materialize, he acknowledged that "the lead was false".

At this point, Dr Jameson-Carr returned from Europe and created another sensation by revealing that, in the days between being thrown off the *Franconia* and her death, Starr had written him three letters, and these made it abundantly clear that she had intended to commit suicide. The first declared that she meant to "end my worthless, disorderly bore of an existence — before I ruin anyone else's life as well." "I take dope to forget, and drink to try and like people." The third letter, posted shortly before she left home for the last time, said that she intended to be successful this time (it emerged that she had made an earlier suicide attempt in London), and described how she intended to eat a large final meal, with plenty of alcohol (she was always worried about gaining weight), then kill herself. "I am going to enjoy my last cigarettes. I won't worry because men flirt with me in the streets — I shall encourage them — I don't care who they are. I'm afraid I've always been a rotten 'sleeper'; it's the preliminaries that count with me."

That seemed to settle the matter; Starr *must* have committed suicide. But why at Long Beach? Why wearing only a dress? Why by lying down in the water — as the sand in her lungs suggested — rather than jumping off a bridge or a quay?

In 1948, Morris Markey, a journalist who had worked on the case and become a friend of the Faithfulls, unveiled his own theory on the case. Starr, he believed, *had* left home determined to commit suicide, and had eaten her final meal as planned, although without much alcohol. Then she had picked up a man and gone to the beach with him. As on the previous occasion with the ex-soldier, she had declined sexual intercourse at the last minute, and the man had handled her roughly and raped her. Then, afraid of going to jail, he had drowned her, and walked away through the shallows to avoid leaving footprints.

The theory seems far-fetched — that she was murdered when she set out to commit suicide — yet it covers all the facts, and explains the puzzle of the male semen inside her.

Tucker Faithfull, Starr's chain-smoking younger sister, became a celebrity after Starr's death, with offers of nightclub engagements and movie parts. She loved the limelight, but two weeks after her sister's death, startled reporters with a sudden outburst: "I'm not sorry she's dead. Everybody's happier. She made life miserable."

The weekend Starr died, Tucker was spending a dirty weekend with a lover named Jones; she had pawned her fake leopardskin coat to pay her train fare, and had to borrow $5 to get home when Jones declined to give it to her.

She married a lawyer in 1937.

A modern criminologist might suggest another solution: that Starr had taken a large dose of veronal and lay down on the beach to wait for the tide to come in; some passing beachcomber had found her — either before or after death — and had intercourse with her. The bruises on her arms could have been caused as her body was pounded by waves — a body will bruise for some time after death. If this theory is correct, then Starr committed suicide as she intended.

On the whole, these theories are probably as close as anyone will ever come to solving the mystery of the death of Starr Faithfull.

The Evangelista Murders

On the morning of 3 July 1929 Vincent Elias, a dealer in real estate, called at the house of Benjamino Evangelista. Evangelista, or Benny Evangelist as he preferred to be known, was a repair and building contractor who lived in one of the poorer districts of Detroit. Elias arrived at Evangelista's three-storey house at about 10.30, and finding that his knocking brought no reply he decided to enter and investigate. Seeing that the foyer was empty, Elias opened the door of Evangelista's office and walked into a scene that resembled an abattoir. Evangelista was slumped in his chair, surrounded and covered with blood. On the floor next to his body was his head, cleanly removed. The visitor fled to summon the police.

Soon patrolmen Costage and Lawrence arrived at the scene, and they continued the grisly investigation. Among the gore in Evangelista's office were two unused swords, a false beard and wig, and a notched staff. Also, on the floor near the severed head were photographs of a child in a coffin. Bloody footprints led to the stairs.

In the upstairs bedroom the shocked patrolmen found Evangelista's wife and youngest child, a baby. The mother had been almost beheaded, and her arm nearly severed, while the baby had been killed by multiple head wounds. In the adjoining room were the elder children's beds, two daughters of four and six, both decapitated, with some attempt to detach the arm of one of them. Finally the eldest daughter, an eight-year-old, was lying in the doorway to the landing, also hacked to death. Unlike Evangelista, who was fully clothed, the upstairs victims were in their night attire. Only the eldest daughter seemed to have had time to react to the murderer, having put on her bathrobe and made for her mother's bedroom.

Another bloody footprint descended the stairs, and a fingerprint of a left thumb, also in blood, was left on the latch of the outer door. What other evidence was left pointing to the identity of the killer will never be known, as the Detroit police failed to properly document or preserve any other physical evidence. Within hours the Evangelista home was packed with police and journalists, attracted not only by the gruesome and terrible aspect of the murders, but also by what the police discovered in the Evangelista cellar.

"Benny Evangelist", apart from being a building contractor, was a local faith healer. People paid high prices to receive cures from the "wise man". Despite this fundamentally unchristian sideline, the whole Evangelista family regularly attended the local Catholic church and seemed at least averagely devout. Both the police and the local people were thus surprised to find that Benny seemed to be the head of a pagan cult. His cellar was decorated like a temple, with the walls and ceiling draped with green cloth and an altar at one end. Above the altar were hung models of hellish demons, made from papier mache with dog hair glued onto them. An outward-facing sign in the basement window read "The Great Celestial Planet Exhibition". Among the papers removed by the police from Evangelista's office was a "Bible" of this cult titled *The Oldest History of the World, Discovered By Occult Science In Detroit, Michigan*". It was to run to four volumes, but only the first volume seems to have reached print. The book was a long and bloody story of prehistoric humanity, not unlike the Old Testament in style. There were many episodes of occult magic and royal intrigue. The principal character of the *History* is the Prophet Meil. Possibly Evangelista identified himself with Meil, as the staff found in his office was very similar to the one that the Prophet is described as carrying. The cultists who believed the details of the *History* called themselves The Great Union Federation of America.

The preface describes how the book came to be written: that it took exactly twenty years to write, from 2 February 1906 to 2 February 1926, and that the story came to the author in visions every night between midnight and 3 a.m. It was during this period, the police were later to establish, that the murders took place.

Also found among Evangelista's belongings were many items of female underwear, each labeled with the owner's name. Carried away, perhaps, by the occult atmosphere of the investigation, the police concluded that they were used for psychometry, the art of locating people through psychic impressions gained from their belongings.

Although their crime-scene investigations had been worse than useless, the Detroit police tried hard to find witnesses or dig up connections. The investigation reached the conclusion that the last person to see Evangelista alive was a local called Umberto Tecchio. Together with a friend, Tecchio had visited Evangelista at his house the evening before the murder to deliver the final payment on a house. However there was no mention of a completed sale in any of Evangelista's papers. Suspecting that Tecchio had been cheated by Evangelista and had wreaked bloody revenge, the police searched Tecchio's rooming house. In the barn below the house police found a dull axe, a sharp banana knife and a newly cleaned pair of shoes.

This evidence seemed hopeful, so the police next questioned Tecchio's room-mate Angelo Depoli. He was uncommunicative and surly to such an extent that the police bad-temperedly set immigration on him. As it turned out Depoli was an illegal immigrant, and was deported. With him went any hope of establishing Tecchio's movements on the night of the murder.

Umberto Tecchio was certainly a violent man. His first wife had divorced him for knifing her brother to death. When she gained possession of the house and lived there with her new husband, Tecchio threatened to blow them up. Several days later the new husband was shot dead on the steps of his house. The police, apparently for reasons of leniency, ruled it a suicide. Also, just after the murders, police received a tip that a newspaper boy had seen Tecchio standing on the porch of Evangelista's house smoking a cigarette at 5 a.m. on the morning after the murders.

Unsolved Crimes

Officers sent to find the newspaper boy were told he was dead.

There were other possibilities for violence revealed by police researching Evangelista's background. He had moved from Naples to live with his brother in Pennsylvania. His brother had eventually thrown him out of the house for his occult interests. Before moving to Michigan, Evangelista had lived in York, Pennsylvania, an area renowned for its occult sub-community. While living there he was friendly with Aurelius Angelino, a chief cultist, who was put in a mental asylum for killing two of his family and wounding the others with an axe in an attempt to dispose of them all. Police seemed so taken with this connection that they exhumed Evangelista in order to check his fingerprints. Exactly how he could have beheaded himself after killing his family was never fully explained by the police.

In the absence of any meaningful connections with York cultists, police researched the other possible source of suspects: Evangelista's reputed connection with the Black Hand, an extortion organization. Local sources reported that Evangelista delivered threats for the Black Hand. A retribution killing had taken place across the street from Evangelista's house early in 1926. At the time the police had known who the gunman was, but despairing of ever convicting him, they allowed him to flee to avoid further violence. The gunman's name was Louis Evangelist. Feeling that Evangelista may have had some connection with this killing police tracked down Evangelist to a railroad track-laying gang near Pittsburgh, but he seemed to know nothing of the subsequent murders.

Evangelista *had* received a death threat from the Black Hand; it was found among his papers dated roughly a year before the killings. There was also an unposted letter by Evangelista saying that a job had been bungled before and that a certain unnamed threat might have to be removed.

Intriguing though these things are, they provide no real evidence or even solid theory.

The murder investigation foundered, and remained unsolved on the Detroit police files. However information about the murders kept surfacing, a piece at a time.

A Mrs Emmanuel Maiccucci came forward to say that the Evangelistas had owned two machetes that had been missing from the scene. Mrs Maiccucci was the wife of Umberto Tecchio who had divorced him for the murder of her brother. She said that while she had been married to Tecchio he had taken her to Evangelista to cure an illness. She had noticed the machetes during her cure.

A young man came forward to say that he had been the newspaper boy who had seen Tecchio on the Evangelistas' porch. He told police that after he had realized what had gone on that night he had avoided the house for years, never passing it and too afraid to come forward.

Tecchio's fellow guests at the rooming-house said that they were not sure whether Tecchio had come home at all on the night of the murders.

The reason for the sudden increase in information was simple: Tecchio had died. Whatever conclusions the police came to it was clear that many people in the local neighbourhood had been too afraid of Tecchio to reveal all that they knew. The existence of the newspaper boy had been hidden by the whole community. Some local people must have thought that Tecchio was the murderer.

However, the murders remain unsolved. There is no doubt that this has a lot to do with the incredible incompetence of the Detroit police. They deported their most valuable witness and when they later came to test the fingerprint on the latch against Tecchio's prints, many policemen came to the conclusion that the mark had been made by an investigating officer.

The theories about the motive and murderer are varied and in some cases quite plausible. The photographs of the child in a coffin suggest to some people that Evangelista had failed to cure someone and that, in pagan tradition, he was put to death for the death of his patient. Another theory points out that Aurelius Angelino, the York cultist, had escaped from his asylum at the time of the murders, and that he, like the person who left the thumbprint on the latch, was left-handed. The main police theories, concerning the Black Hand and Umberto Tecchio, are to some degree tenable, but really do not justify such cold-blooded and wholesale violence.

In the end, the cult connections are the most gripping if not the most plausible source of explanations. Was Evangelista's cult connected to a more widespread network of believers? The title "The Great Union Federation of America" tends to suggest it was. Did Evangelista somehow compromise or annoy a nationwide group of cultists and was ritualistically punished for it? It seems that the facts are destined to remain unknown.

Wrongful arrest

In 1930, an American actor called Philip Yale Drew came close to being hanged for a murder he did not commit.

At 6.15 on the evening of Saturday, 22 June, 1929, Mrs Annie Oliver returned to the tobacconist's shop where she had left her husband, Alfred Oliver, serving a customer. She found him dying behind the counter, and when she asked him what had happened, he said: 'My dear, I don't know.' He died twenty-four hours later.

There were no clues, and two months later, the investigation had dragged to a halt. Then, in August, Chief Constable Thomas Burrows was having a drink in the Wellington Club, opposite the Royal County Theatre when another member commented to him: 'That chap

you're looking for is Yale Drew, the actor fellow who
was in *The Monster*.'

Drew was arrested in Nottingham, where his company
was acting, and a pair of his trousers — apparently bloodstained — was taken away. A woman who had been
standing near Oliver's shop, in Cross Street, insisted that
she had seen Drew wiping blood from his face shortly after
the time of the murder. Drew insisted that he did not even
know where Cross Street was. When another witness said
that they had heard him say he was going to Cross Street to
get a newspaper, Drew insisted that what he had said was
that he was going 'across the street' to get a newspaper.

Two witnesses who said they had seen him near the shop
were taken to Nottingham, and asked to pick out Drew as
he walked along the street. Both of them did so. But then,
Drew was extremely well known in Reading, so this proved
nothing.

The inquest — which was, in effect, Philip Yale Drew's
murder trial, opened on 9 October, 1929, in the Small
Town Hall. It was obvious that the evidence against Drew
was entirely circumstantial — people who claimed they had
seen him, or someone like him, near the scene of the
murder. But things began to swing in Drew's favour when
a butcher's assistant named Alfred Wells came to give his
evidence. He had formerly told the police that, on the day
of the murder, he had seen a man resembling Drew in
Cross Street — a man who carried his raincoat across his
shoulder, as Drew did. But when a journalist named
Bernard O'Donnell introduced Wells to Drew, Wells
immediately said that this was not the man he had
seen. He had spoken to him, and the man had a north
country accent. He declared that he had told the police
that the man he had seen was not Drew.

The police denied this — and then were forced to
withdraw their denial when Well's statement was found
among a pile of papers.

The jury brought in a verdict of murder by person or persons unknown, and Drew walked out of the court a free man.

The solution to the mystery almost certainly lies in the fact that Saturday 22 June was always referred to in Reading as Black Saturday, because it was the day that the town was invaded by race gangs attracted by the annual Ascot and Windsor race meetings. It seems more likely that the unknown killer of Alfred Oliver was among these louts and roughs, rather than a well known actor with two bank accounts, both in credit.

The Cleveland Torso Killer

On a warm September afternoon in 1935, two boys on their way home from school walked along a dusty, sooty gully called Kingsbury Run, in the heart of Cleveland, Ohio. On a weed-covered slope known as Jackass Hill, one challenged the other to a race, and they hurtled sixty feet down the slope to the bottom. Sixteen-year-old James Wagner was the winner, and as he halted, panting, he noticed something white in the bushes a few yards away. A closer look revealed that it was a naked body, and that it was headless.

The police who arrived soon after found the body of a young white male clad only in black socks; the genitals had also been removed. It lay on its back, with the legs stretched out and the arms placed neatly by the sides, as if laid out for a funeral. Thirty feet away, the policemen found another body, lying in the same position; it was of an older man, and had also been decapitated and emasculated.

Hair sticking out of the ground revealed one of the heads a few yards away, and the second was found nearby. The genitals were also found lying nearby, as if thrown away by the killer.

One curious feature of the case was that there was no blood on the ground or on the bodies, which were quite clean. It looked as if they had been killed and beheaded elsewhere, then carefully washed when they had ceased to bleed.

Medical examination made the case more baffling than ever. The older corpse was badly decomposed, and the skin discoloured; the pathologists discovered that this was due to some chemical substance, as if the killer had tried to preserve the body. The older victim had been dead about two weeks. The younger man had only been dead three days. His fingerprints enabled the police to identify him as twenty-eight-year-old Edward Andrassy, who had a minor police record for carrying concealed weapons. He lived near Kingsbury Run and had a reputation as a drunken brawler.

But the most chilling discovery was that Andrassy had been killed by decapitation. Rope marks on his wrists revealed that he had been tied and had struggled violently. The killer had apparently cut off his head with a knife. The skill with which the operation had been performed suggested a butcher — or possibly a surgeon.

It proved impossible to identify the older man. But the identification of Andrassy led the police to hope that it should not be too difficult to trace his killer. He had spent his nights gambling and drinking in a slum part of town and was known as a pimp. But further investigation also revealed that he had male lovers. Lead after lead looked marvellously promising. The husband of a married woman with whom he had had an affair had sworn to kill him. But the man was able to prove his innocence. So were various shady characters who might have borne a grudge. Lengthy police investigation led to a dead end — as it did in another ten cases of the killer who became known as "the Mad Butcher of Kingsbury Run".

Four months later, on a raw January Sunday, the howling of a dog finally led a black woman resident of East

Twentieth Street — not far from Kingsbury Run — to go and investigate. She found the chained animal trying to get at a basket near a factory wall. Minutes later, she told a neighbour that the basket contained "hams". But the neighbour soon recognized the "hams" as parts of a human arm. A burlap bag proved to contain the lower half of a female torso. The head was missing, as were the left arm and lower parts of both legs. But fingerprints again enabled the police to trace the victim, who had a record for soliciting. She proved to be a forty-one-year-old prostitute named Florence Polillo, a squat, double-chinned woman who was well known in the bars of the neighbourhood.

Again, there were plenty of leads, and again, all of them petered out. Two weeks later, the left arm and lower legs were found in a vacant lot. The head was never recovered.

The murder of Flo Polillo raised an unwelcome question. The first two murders had convinced the police that they were looking for a homosexual sadist; this latest crime made it look as if this killer was quite simply a sadist — like Peter Kurten, the Dusseldorf killer, executed in 1931; he had killed men, women and children indifferently, and he was not remotely homosexual. And now the pathologist recalled that, a year before the first double murder, the torso of an unknown woman had been found on the edge of Lake Erie. It began to look as if the Mad Butcher was quite simply a sadist.

At least the Cleveland public felt they had one thing in their favour. Since the double killing, the famous Eliot Ness had been appointed Cleveland's Director of Public Safety. Ness and his "Untouchables" had cleared up Chicago's Prohibition rackets, then, in 1934, Ness had moved to Cleveland to fight its gangsters. With Ness in charge, the Head Hunter of Kingsbury Run — another press sobriquet — would find himself becoming the hunted.

But it was soon clear to Ness that hunting a sadistic pervert is nothing like hunting professional gangsters. The killer struck at random, and unless he was careless enough to leave behind a clue — like a fingerprint — then the only hope of catching him was in the act. And Ness soon became convinced that the Mad Butcher took great pleasure in feeling that he was several steps ahead of the police.

The Head Hunter waited until the summer before killing again, then lived up to his name by leaving the head of a young man, wrapped in a pair of trousers, under a bridge in Kingsbury Run; again, two boys found it on 22 June 1936. The body was found a quarter of a mile away, and it was obvious from the blood that he had died where he lay. And medical evidence showed that he had died from decapitation — it was not clear how the killer had prevented him from struggling while he did it. The victim was about twenty-five, and heavily tattooed. His fingerprints were not in police files. Three weeks later, a young female hiker discovered another decapitated body in a gully; the head lay nearby. The decomposition made it clear that this man had been killed before the previously-discovered victim.

The last "Butchery" of 1936 was of another man of about thirty, found in Kingsbury Run; the body had been amputated in two, and emasculated. A hat found nearby led to a partial identification: a housewife recalled giving it to a young tramp. Not far away there was a "hobo camp" where down-and-outs slept; this was obviously where the Butcher had found his latest victim.

The fact that Cleveland had been the scene of a Republican Convention and was now the site of a "Great Expo", led to even more frantic police activity and much press criticism. The murders were reported all over the world and, in Nazi Germany and Fascist Italy, were cited as proof of the decadence of the New World.

As month after month went by with no further grisly discoveries, Clevelanders hoped they had heard the last of the Mad Butcher. But in February 1937, that hope was dashed when the killer left the body of a young woman in a chopped-up pile on the shores of Lake Erie. She was never identified. The eighth victim, a young negress, *was* identified from her teeth as Mrs Rose Wallace, forty; only the skeleton remained, and it looked as if she may have been killed in the previous year.

Victim No. nine was male and had been dismembered; when he was fished out of the river, the head was missing, and was never found. This time the killer had gone even further in his mutilations — like Jack the Ripper. It was impossible to identify the victim. Two men seen in a boat were thought to be the Butcher with an accomplice, but this suggestion that there might be two Butchers led nowhere.

The Butcher now seems to have taken a rest until nine months later. Then the lower part of a leg was pulled out of the river. Three weeks later, two burlap bags in the river proved to contain more body-fragments, which enabled the pathologist to announce that the victim was female, a brunette of about twenty-five. She was never identified.

The killer was to strike twice more. More than a year after the last discovery, in August 1938, the dismembered torso of a woman was found on a dump on the lakefront, and a search of the area revealed the bones of a second victim, a male. A quilt in which the remains of this twelfth victim were wrapped was identified as having been given to a junk man. Neither body could be identified.

One thing was now obvious: the Butcher was selecting his victims from vagrants and down-and-outs. Ness decided to take the only kind of action that seemed left to him: two days after the last find, police raided the "shantytown" near Kingsbury Run, arrested hundreds of vagrants, and burned it down. Whether or not by coincidence, the murders now ceased.

The suspects. Two of the most efficient of the manhunters, Detectives Merylo and Zalewski, had spent a great deal of time searching for the killer's "laboratory". At one point they thought they had found it — but, like all leads, this one faded away.

Next the investigators discovered that Flo Polillo and Rose Wallace — Victim No. eight — had frequented the same saloon, and that Andrassy — No. two — had been a "regular" there too. They also learned of a middle-aged man called Frank who carried knives and threatened people with them when drunk. When they learned that this man — Frank Dolezal — had also been living with Flo Polillo, they felt they had finally identified the killer. Dolezal was arrested, and police discovered a brown substance like dried blood in the cracks of his bathroom floor. Knives with dried blood-stains on them provided further incriminating evidence. Under intensive questioning, Dolezal — a bleary-eyed, unkempt man — confessed to the murder of Flo Polillo. Newspapers announced the capture of the Butcher. Then things began to go wrong. The "dried blood" in the bathroom proved not to be blood after all. Dolezal's "confession" proved to be full of errors about the corpse and method of disposal. And when, in August 1939, Dolezal hanged himself in jail, the autopsy revealed that he had two cracked ribs, and suggested that his confession had been obtained by force.

Yet Ness himself claimed that he knew the solution to the murders. He reasoned that the killer was a man who had a house of his own in which to dismember the bodies, and a car in which to transport them. So he was not a down-and-out. The skill of the mutilations suggested medical training. The fact that some of the victims had been strong men suggested that the Butcher had to be big and powerful — a conclusion supported by a size twelve footprint near one of the bodies.

Ness set three of his top agents, Virginia Allen, Barney Davis and Jim Manski, to make enquiries among the upper levels of Cleveland society. Virginia was a sophisticated girl with contacts among Cleveland socialites. And it was she

81

who learned about a man who sounded like the ideal suspect. Ness was to call him "Gaylord Sundheim" — a big man from a well-to-do family, who had a history of psychiatric problems. He had also studied medicine. When the three "Untouchables" called on him, he leered sarcastically at Virginia and closed the door in their faces. Ness invited him — pressingly — to lunch, and he came under protest. When Ness finally told him he suspected him of being the Butcher — hoping that shock tactics might trigger a confession — "Sundheim" sneered: "Prove it".

Soon after this, "Sundheim" had himself committed to a mental institution. Ness knew *he* was now "untouchable", for even if Ness could prove his guilt, he could plead insanity.

During the next two years Ness received a series of jeering postcards, some signed "Your paranoid nemesis". They ceased abruptly when "Sundheim" died in the mental institution.

Was "Sundheim" the Butcher? Probably. But not certainly. In Pittsburgh in 1940, three decapitated bodies were found in old boxcars (railway coaches). Members of Ness's team went to investigate, but no clue to the treble murder was ever discovered. The case remains unsolved.

Who Killed Kennedy?

At 12.30 p.m. on 2 November 1963, President John F. Kennedy was travelling through Dallas, Texas, in the back of an open limousine, with his wife beside him and Governor John B. Connally and Connally's wife in front of them. As the motorcade passed the Texas School Book Depository in Dealey Plaza, shots rang out and the President clutched his neck with both hands and slumped in his seat. A second bullet caused his head to "explode".

Connally was also struck by a bullet. Jackie Kennedy cried: "They've killed my husband . . . I have his brains in my hand!"

The Secret Service ordered the car to drive at top speed to the Parkland Memorial Hospital. But despite all efforts to save him, the President died shortly afterwards. A bullet that later became known as Exhibit 399 was found on the stretcher.

The police had pinpointed the Book Depository as the source of the shots. Near a window on the sixth floor, they found three empty cartridge cases. A few minutes after the shooting, a motorcycle policeman was talking to the superintendent of the building when a man named Lee Harvey Oswald walked out of the elevator on the second floor. The policeman asked the superintendent: "Do you know this man?", and the superintendent said: "Yes, he works here." Oswald was allowed to walk out of the building.

Half an hour or so after the assassination, Oswald was walking down the street when police officer J. D. Tippit, driving a patrol car, called him over. Oswald spoke to him calmly then began to walk away. Tippit jumped from the car and ran after him; Oswald turned, pulled out a revolver, and shot Tippit dead, moving close to him to fire the final shot.

An hour later, a ticket seller at the Texas Theater saw Oswald walk in without buying a ticket; she called the police. As they approached Oswald he pointed his gun and pulled the trigger; it misfired. Moments later he was in custody. Soon after, news bulletins announced the arrest of a suspect.

Oswald was an ex-marine who had defected to the USSR and married a Russian girl. Refused a residence permit he had returned to the USA in June 1962. In March 1963 he had purchased a rifle with a telescopic sight from a mail order firm — his original intention was to assassinate a retired army general. He had moved to Dallas after further unsuccessful attempts to emigrate to Russia and Cuba, and had found a job in the Book Depository. It seems that when he learned from newspaper reports that the President would be visiting Dallas, and saw that the route passed below the Book Depository, he made plans to kill Kennedy.

The rifle with the telescopic sight was found on the sixth floor of the Book Depository, and one of Oswald's palm prints was found on it. He denied killing the President and Officer Tippit, and answered questions "arrogantly".

At 11.20 on Saturday, 24 November 1963, Oswald was being taken from the Dallas Police Headquarters to a car waiting outside, and crowds of photographers — including television crews — were taking pictures, when a man stepped forward, jammed a revolver against Oswald's chest, and pulled the trigger. The man was grabbed by a policeman as Oswald collapsed. Newsmen yelled to ask his name, and the man shouted back: "I'm Jack Ruby — you know me."

Oswald was rushed to Parkland Hospital and operated on by the same surgeon who had tried to save Kennedy's life. But by 1.07 he was pronounced dead.

Ruby was a Dallas nightclub owner who had many friends in the police force — as well as gangland connections. Witnesses reported that he had been behaving oddly since Kennedy's assassination, and his charlady mentioned that he had been talking to himself on the morning he killed Oswald. Tried for murder in 1964, Ruby was sentenced to death, but died of cancer in 1967, before the sentence could be carried out.

To large numbers of Americans, it seemed too convenient that Kennedy's assassin had been killed within two days, and that Oswald's killer had had so little trouble in shooting him. There was soon talk of conspiracy. This began when a film taken by a local business man, Abraham Zapruder, was examined frame by frame, and seemed to show that the first shot caused Kennedy's head to jerk *backwards* — although the Book Depository was behind him. This led to the belief that there was a second gunman *ahead* of the President, on a grassy knoll, and that Oswald had, in fact, shot at Kennedy, but had probably missed. (In the Marine Corps, Oswald's appalling marksmanship had been a joke.) The Zapruder film seemed to indicate that at least four shots, not three, had been fired. Examination of the wounds suggested that Connally had been hit by the same bullet that passed through Kennedy's neck.

A woman named Julia Mercer testified that she was driving through Dealey Plaza an hour and a half before the assassination when she saw a green truck parked with two tyres on the kerb. A man she later identified as Oswald got out with a rifle and went towards the grassy knoll. She looked back at the driver, and later identified him as Jack Ruby.

Another popular conspiracy theory was that Vice President Lyndon Johnson — who had won Texas for the Democrats by a narrow majority — had planned the assassination in order to become president. A libellous play called *Macbird*, based on this theory, had a long run on Broadway.

FBI Director J. Edgar Hoover was another candidate for the role of paymaster of the assassin. He disliked Kennedy, and disliked his brother Robert — the Attorney General — even more. Robert Kennedy was speaking of an all-out war on the Mafia with his own Justice Department, challenging Hoover's long-established supremacy.

Another conspiracy theory declared that the CIA was responsible — Kennedy's own intelligence agency — because there was a feeling of anger about the incompetence of the Bay of Pigs invasion of Cuba. Many theories include heavy involvement with Cuban anti-Castro exiles — Oswald himself had attempted to join an anti-Castro group in Miami a few months before the assassination. One view holds that he was trying to infiltrate the group for his Communist masters, another that he joined the assassination conspiracy on behalf of Cuban exiles who felt betrayed by Kennedy.

One of the members of an anti-Castro group was an ultra-conservative named David Ferrie, a completely hairless character (he suffered from a disease called alopecia) who glued bits of orange hair to his head and eyebrows. Ferrie called himself "Dr" as well as "Bishop", and had lost his job as an airline pilot because of his sexual preference for boys. His hatred of Kennedy was almost pathological. He had been a boyhood friend of Oswald, and was seen with him shortly before the assassination.

In the mid-1960s, the New Orleans District Attorney Jim Garrison alleged that Ferrie, Oswald and a businessman called Clay Shaw had been behind the assassination. But a few days after Garrison announced his findings to the press, Ferrie's naked body was found in his apartment, together with two suicide notes. Cause of death was listed as a brain haemorrhage, possibly brought on by an unknown poison. The same day, Ferrie's close anti-Castro associate Eladio del Valle was murdered in Miami, shot through the heart — his killer was never found. The only man to go on trial was Clay Shaw, but the evidence against him was negligible, and he was found not guilty.

Perhaps more convincing than any of these theories is the argument that Kennedy was murdered by the Mafia, on whom he — via his brother Robert — had declared war. In the 1950s, Robert Kennedy had served on a senate committee whose aim was to expose Mafia involvement with the Teamsters' Union, headed by Jimmy Hoffa. Kennedy's father Joe Kennedy is alleged to have been in partnership with gangster Frank Costello in the bootleg era. Sam Giancana, the Chicago mob boss, was actually sharing a bedfellow, Judith Exner, with the President, who was a notorious womanizer. It was alleged that Kennedy was supplied with ladyfriends by Frank Sinatra, a friend of Giancana and other Mafia figures, and that Kennedy's affair with Marilyn Monroe originated in his Sinatra connection. The aim of Giancana may have been to exert pressure on the Kennedy brothers to soften their stance towards the mob. Giancana also believed that he was basically responsible for Kennedy's election as President, since he had "delivered" a vital Chicago vote in the 1960 election — a vote without which Kennedy's bid for the presidency would have been stillborn. Carlos Marcello, a New Orleans Mafia boss who was also being hounded by Robert Kennedy, is reported to have said that Robert Kennedy would be "taken care of" by the killing of his brother the President. "When attacked by a dog, it is no good cutting off the tail. Cut off the head and the dog is out of business."

Significantly, Jack Ruby was born in Chicago, and as a teenager worked for Al Capone as a delivery boy. There is some evidence that it was the Chicago "mob" that placed Ruby in Dallas — his task being to run a restaurant as a front for Syndicate business. A 1956 FBI report mentioned him as a mob contact. Just before the assassination, Ruby was in deep financial trouble, owing the government $60,000 in taxes. Then he suddenly told his lawyer that his problems had been miraculously solved. At about this time, he is known to have had many meetings with old mob acquaintances.

Shortly after Ruby's trial in 1964, Chief Justice Earl Warren, president of the Warren Commission charged with investigating the Kennedy assassination, and Congressman Gerald Ford — the future President — went to Dallas to interview Ruby. Ruby told them that he would have to be taken to Washington before he could answer their questions freely. "I want to tell the truth, and I can't tell it here." He said later: "I have been used as a scapegoat."

When the Warren Report on the assassination was published in 1979, it concluded that all the evidence suggested that Oswald had acted alone in killing Kennedy. It could very well be that this simple solution is indeed the final truth. But, three decades after the assassination, there are certainly very few people who would accept that conclusion.

Chapter Four

British Enigmas

To return to Britain after studying American homicide is like returning to the country after a month in a busy metropolis. The scale of events is somehow smaller. Having said that, it must be admitted that the scale of incompetence in some classic English mysteries is awe-inspiring. For example, in the case that has become known as the Croydon poisonings, one simple blunder on the part of the pathologist guaranteed that a murderer — or murderess — would never be brought to justice.

It must be admitted that most British murders of the twentieth century lack the element of mystery — there is not a single one, with the exception of the Luard case (see page 29), in which the motive is not crudely obvious. The Wallace case, which took place in Liverpool in 1931, is the exception. And in spite of recent evidence which seems to point towards a solution, it retains the tantalizing quality of one of the great unsolved mysteries.

A unique case is the Harry Whitecliffe mystery because it does not reside in the question "Who killed so-and-so", but in the precise identity of a man who is alleged to be a mass murderer.

The Case of the Croydon Poisonings

The London suburb of Croydon has always been a quiet and respectable area — one in which the scandals tend to be of the domestic rather than criminal variety. Yet, in the early months of 1929, this peaceful back-water was discovered to be the scene of what was to become one of the most notorious cases of mass poisoning in British legal history.

In April 1928, Edmund Creighton Duff was living with his wife Grace and their three children at 16 South Park Road, Croydon. At fifty-nine, Duff, a retired British Resident in the civil service of Northern Nigeria and veteran of the Boer War, was supplementing his modest pension by working at a City firm of paper manufacturers and indulging in the odd financial investment. He was a jovial and well-liked man – nicknamed "Major Duff" by his friends – who gave the impression of exceptional fitness and robust constitution.

Thus, while enjoying a spring fishing trip, he was disturbed to find he was running a fever. He returned home early and complained of it to his wife, but she paid it little heed; he had a tendency to over-react on the rare occasions he felt under the weather. Despite the fever he ate a supper of chicken and vegetables and washed it down with bottled beer. Shortly afterwards he complained of severe stomach-ache and, on his way to bed, of leg cramps. During the night his condition worsened and a physician, Dr John Binning, was called to attend him.

Binning diagnosed colic, but as Duff worsened he realized it was something far more dangerous. He and his partner, Dr Robert Elwell, fought hard to keep their patient alive, but at 11.20 p.m. on the evening after his return from his fishing trip, Edmund Duff died in agony.

The two doctors were at a loss to explain their patient's death and so were legally unable to sign the death certificate; in such circumstances an inquest is automatically carried out. Despite the fact that Duff had exhibited all the major symptoms of arsenic poisoning, neither doctor was inclined to follow this suggestion to its logical conclusion. They were both friends of the Duffs – Dr Elwell especially, who liked to half-jokingly flirt with Grace Duff – and understandably dismissed the possibility of murder.

Practically everybody but his closest friends and a few reporters are convinced that Richard John Bingham Lucan, seventh earth of Lucan, is a murderer. The evidence is strong that on the chilly night of 7 November, 1974, John Lucan burst into the expensive London townhouse occupied by his estranged wife and children, attacked and injured his wife, and killed, probably by accident, the children's nanny, Sandra Rivett. The mystery is that Lord Lucan then disappeared, and though he was one of the most sought-after men in the world, no trace of him has ever been found.

The pathologist who performed the autopsy, Dr Robert Bronte, reported to the coroner's inquest that the body showed no sign of the ingestion of arsenic. He attributed the death to a heart attack brought on by sunstroke sustained on the fishing trip. In the light of subsequent events this autopsy report was rather amazing to say the least; Dr Bronte had made a misjudgment of staggering proportions. If he had conducted the autopsy more thoroughly a murder enquiry would have ensued and, quite possibly, two lives would have been saved.

Duff's funeral was, of course, attended by his wife's family; her mother, the rather imperious Mrs Violet Emilia Sidney, her younger sister Miss Vera Sidney — unmarried and at forty, a boisterous good-natured woman and the apple of her mother's eye — and her brother Thomas Sidney, a professional entertainer.

Although not noticeably well-to-do the Sidneys were an upper class family and highly respected in the local community. They were a close-knit, not to say clannish family, and Edmund had always been treated as a bit of an outsider. In fact, there had been some friction between Edmund Duff and the Sidneys. Mrs Sidney had felt Duff to be rather too lower class and underpaid for her daughter — especially after he lost £5,000 of Grace's money on a bad investment. The abrasively humorous Tom Sidney considered Edmund too stuffy and often made jokes at his expense. It was also suggested, after the discovery of the murders, that Duff had had an affair with Tom's attractive American wife, Margaret. Even so, the idea of any foul-play involved in his death had, as yet, occurred to nobody.

On 11 February 1929, almost a year after the death, Vera Sidney — Grace's younger sister — complained of feeling off-colour. This in itself was unusual since she generally refused to "give in" to sicknesses and thought little of those that did. In fact she was not the only person in Violet Sidney's house who felt ill that day. The maid, Kate Noakes, and the family cat were also ill. The connecting factor was the soup all three had eaten at lunchtime.

Vera rallied a couple of days later, as did the maid and cat, but then made the mistake of taking the soup again for lunch, this time joined by her Aunt Gwen. Both became ill, but only Vera was seriously affected. Again doctors Binning and Elwell were called. This time they were unwilling to take any chances and brought in a stomach specialist. He diagnosed intestinal influenza.

Vera died in great pain on 15 February, four days after she was first taken ill. Again, the possibility of murder was still not considered by the family physicians despite the fact that she had displayed virtually the same symptoms of arsenic poisoning as had Edmund Duff.

Violet Sidney was shattered by her daughter's death and her family feared that the old lady might die of the shock. Doctor Elwell prescribed her a strengthening tonic to be taking before meals and she started to slowly recover. Then, on 5 March 1929, she took her tonic, ate her lunch and became very ill. In her lucid moments she insisted that she had been poisoned. The tonic had tasted oddly gritty and bitter and she was convinced that something had been added to it. The already weakened, seventy-year-old lady died within hours, once again displaying the symptoms of arsenic poisoning.

This time even Elwell and Binning could not ignore the evidence and refused to sign the death certificate. Even so, Violet Sidney had been laid to rest by the time the Home Office decided to make enquiries; so she had to be disinterred, along with her daughter and later her son-in-law, to be re-examined. This time the autopsies were carried out by Dr Bernard Spilsbury, a brilliant pathologist who did much to advance the field of forensic science. His more expert examination found the bodies to contain up to five grains of arsenic each; more than enough to cause death. At last the murders were out.

The poisonings received much media coverage and people up and down the country followed the reports of the three inquests with avid interest. It seemed clear to most observers that a member of the family or somebody close to it was probably responsible. The chances of an outsider, for whatever reason, being able to administer poison surreptitiously was next to nil.

Edmund Duff, it was reported, had quite probably been poisoned on his return from the fishing trip; most likely administered in his bottled beer. Vera had almost certainly been fed the arsenic in her soup; Violet Sidney never partook of soup and the maid had ineffectively been told she could not have any (let alone give it to the cat). Finally forensic examination indeed found heavy traces of arsenic in Violet's tonic bottle. The likeliest source of the arsenic was deduced to be weedkiller, freely available and present in the houses of all the male participants.

Police conducted a large and exhaustive investigation and the Coroner's Court questioned all possible suspects with great care, but in the end the case came to nothing. The evidence was too scanty to implicate any one person or persons of committing the murders and no solid motive could be attached to any of them. In the end, the three people considered most likely to have been the murderer were Tom Sidney, Grace Duff and, rather weirdly, Violet Sidney, the poisoned mother.

Violet was accused by some of hating Edmund Duff and of somehow getting into his pantry and doctoring a bottle of his beer. Then a year later, mad with guilt, she was said to have poisoned her much loved daughter to punish herself. Finally she committed suicide, revealing as she died that the poison had been in her tonic.

It is probably quite safe to reject this theory completely. Violet was not fond of Duff, but had never shown any sign of virulently hating him. All agreed that her shock and grief over the death of Vera were genuine and finally she had seemed both amazed and affronted when proclaiming that she had been poisoned.

Tom Sidney had some financial motive for killing his sister and mother; he stood to gain about £8,000 (about £180,000 in 1992 currency) from their wills, but at the time of the murders he was doing quite well himself and his finances were on a comfortable upturn. An anonymous letter was sent to the coroner at the time of the inquests claiming that Duff was seeing Tom's wife, but no other evidence was ever found to suggest that he had a reason to kill his stuffy brother-in-law.

The most likely candidate, in fact, was Grace Duff. Outwardly a bright and cheerful woman, she was known by close acquaintances to have dark mood swings and to have resented her husband's overly brutal amorous advances (she complained that he left her covered in bruises). Edmund had been away working in Africa for much of their married life and his retirement and permanent return might have upset the balance of her life. She was highly protective

The first inquest on Edmund Duff, performed immdiately after his death by Dr Patrick Bronte, found that he died of natural causes. When Sir Bernard Spilsbury performed a second inquest, he found that Bronte had left most of the intestines unexamined, and that he had accidentally put back into Duff's body some of the organs from a woman on whom he had been performing an inquest the same day.

of her children and Edmund's dodgy financial deals threatened the future of the whole family. She may have wanted him out of the way so that she might marry Dr Elwell, her flirtatious family physician. It is even possible that she killed him for sleeping with her brother's wife.

Her financial state was improved by her husband's death; in fact she gained enough from his life insurance to buy the house they had previously only rented. Even so, she was still far from being comfortably off; £8,000 might have seemed very tempting and having committed one murder others might have seemed less difficult.

Tom Sidney claimed to have no doubt that Grace was the murderer, and apparently neither did Scotland Yard. He later said that the police suggested that he move as far from Grace as possible, so he took his family to the USA. But we only have his word that this was the case; in the States he was also somewhat safer from British justice if new evidence was uncovered. It had also come to light that Violet's estranged husband, the father of Grace, Tom and Vera, had had an illegitimate son who was said to have resented his father's previous family. There is still no definite proof to connect Grace with the poisonings and in the end she remains merely the most likely of several suspects.

The Wallace Case

William Herbert Wallace seemed to be a completely ordinary little man. The critic James Agate once said of him: "That man was born middle-aged". But the appearance of ordinariness concealed a certain sadness and unfulfilment. Wallace was born in Keswick in the Lake District in 1878, the child of lower middle class parents. But he had an intellectual turn of mind, and when he discovered the *Meditations* of the Roman emperor Marcus Aurelius, decided that he was by nature a stoic — that is, one who doesn't expect much out of life, but who thinks it can be improved by hard work and discipline. Like H. G. Wells's Kipps or Mr Polly — of whom he constantly reminds us — he became a draper's assistant, and found the life just as boring as they did. His quest for adventure took him to India — but still as a draper's assistant — then to Shanghai; he found both places a great disappointment, and inevitably caught a bad dose of dysentery, which further undermined his already delicate constitution. So with his Marcus Aurelius in his pocket he returned to England. He became a Liberal election agent in Yorkshire, and on a holiday in Harrogate, met a mild-looking, dark haired young lady named Julia Thorp. She was undoubtedly cleverer than Wallace; she was well-read, spoke French, played the piano and made excellent sketches. They talked about Marcus Aurelius and other intellectual matters and, in a rather leisurely manner, decided they liked one another enough to get married. They married in 1913 and lived in Harrogate. But in the following year, the outbreak of war cost Wallace his job — political agents were not needed during a war. Fortunately, it also caused many job vacancies, and Wallace soon found employment as an insurance agent in Liverpool, working for the Prudential. They moved into a rather dreary little terrace house in a cul-de-sac called Wolverton Crescent, in the Anfield district. And for the next seventeen years, they

William Herbert Wallace, sentenced to death but later released by the
Court of Appeal.

lived a life of peaceful and rather penurious dullness. Wallace pottered about in a chemical laboratory in his home, and even gave occasional lectures on it at the technical college. He also joined a chess club that met regularly in the City Café in North John Street. Julia read library books and sang at the piano. They had no children and, apparently, no real friends. And although life on less than £4 a week was hardly idyllic, they seemed happy enough.

The evening of 19 January 1931 was chilly and damp, but by seven o'clock, a few members had already arrived at the chess club in the City Café. Shortly after 7.15, the telephone rang. Samuel Beattie, captain of the club, answered it. A man's voice asked for Wallace. Beattie said that Wallace would be in later to play a match, and suggested he ring back. "No, I'm too busy — I have my girl's twenty-first birthday on." The man said his name was Qualtrough, and asked if Beattie could give him a message. Beattie wrote it down. It asked Wallace to go to Qualtrough's home at 25 Menlove Gardens East the following evening at 7.30. It was, said Qualtrough, a matter of business.

Wallace slipped quietly into the club some time before eight. Beattie gave him the message, and Wallace made a note of the address in his diary.

The following evening, Wallace arrived home shortly after six, had "high tea" — a substantial meal — and left the house at a quarter-to-seven. He instructed his wife to bolt the back door after him — that was their usual practice. Julia Wallace, who was suffering from a heavy cold, nevertheless went with him to the back gate and watched him leave. Wallace walked to a tramcar, asked the conductor if it went to Menlove Gardens East, and climbed aboard. The conductor advised him to change trams at Penny Lane, and told Wallace where to get off. The conductor of the second tram advised him to get off at Menlove Gardens West.

Wallace now spent a frustrating half hour or so trying to find Menlove Gardens East. Apparently it did not exist; although there *was* a Menlove Gardens North and a Menlove Gardens West. Wallace decided to call at 25 Menlove Gardens West, just in case Beattie had taken down the address wrongly; but the householder there said he had never heard of a Mr Qualtrough. Wallace tried calling at the house of his superintendent at the Prudential, a Mr Joseph Crew, who lived in nearby Green Lane, but found no one at home. He asked a policeman the way, and remarked on the time: "It's not eight o"clock yet." The policeman said: "It's a quarter to." He called in a general shop, then in a newsagent's, where he borrowed a city directory, which seemed to prove beyond all doubt that Menlove Gardens East did not exist. He even asked the proprietress to look in her accounts book to make sure that there was no such place as Menlove Gardens East. People were to remark later that Wallace seemed determined to make people remember him. Finally, even the pertinacious Wallace gave up, and returned home.

He arrived back at 8.45, and inserted his key into the front door. To his surprise, it seemed to be locked on the inside. He tried the back door; that was also locked. Receiving no reply to his knock, he called on his next-door neighbours, the Johnstons, looking deeply concerned, and asked them if they had heard anything unusual — only a thin partition wall separated them from the Wallaces. They said no. John Johnston suggested that perhaps Wallace should try his own back door key, but advised him to try the front door again. And this time, to Wallace's apparent surprise, it opened. Wallace entered the house, and the Johnstons waited politely. A few moments later, Wallace rushed out, looking shocked. "Come and see — she's been killed." They followed him through to the sitting room or parlour, which was at the back of the house. Julia Wallace was lying on the floor, face downward, and the gash in the back of her head made it clear that she had been the victim of an attack. The floor was spattered with blood. Wallace seemed curiously calm as he lit a gas mantle, walking around the body to do so, then suggested that they should look in the kitchen to see if anything had been taken. There was a lid on the kitchen floor, which Wallace said had been wrenched from a cabinet. He took down the cash box from a shelf, looked inside, and told the Johnstons that he thought about £4 had been taken. Then, at Johnston's suggestion, Wallace went upstairs to see if anything was missing, and came down almost immediately saying: "There's £5 in a jar they haven't taken." At this point, Johnston left to fetch the police. Wallace had a momentary breakdown, putting his hands to his head and sobbing, but quickly recovered himself. Mrs Johnston and Wallace then returned to the sitting room, where Wallace commented: "They've finished her — look at the brains." And indeed, Julia Wallace's brains were oozing onto the floor. Then Wallace said with surprise: "Why, whatever was she doing with her mackintosh and my mackintosh?" There was, in fact, a mackintosh under the body, which Wallace shortly identified as his own.

There was a knock at the door; it proved to be a policeman. Wallace told him about his fruitless search for Qualtrough, then accompanied him upstairs. Constable Williams felt that Wallace seemed "extraordinarily cool and calm". The bedroom seemed to have been disturbed, with pillows lying near the fireplace, but the drawers of the dressing table were closed.

Another policeman arrived; then, just before ten o"clock, Professor J. E. W. MacFall, the professor of forensic medicine at Liverpool University. MacFall concluded that Mrs Wallace had died of a violent blow, or blows, to the back left hand side of the skull, and deduced that she had been sitting in an armchair, leaning forward as if talking to somebody, when the blow had been struck. She had fallen to the floor, and the attacker had rained about eleven more blows on her. He also reached the interesting conclusion that Mrs Wallace had died about four hours earlier — that is, at six o'clock.

This, it later proved, was impossible, for the fourteen-year-old milk boy, Alan Close, was to testify that he had delivered a can of milk at 6.25, and that it had been taken in by Mrs Wallace, who advised him to hurry home because he had a cough.

But MacFall had planted suspicion of Wallace in the minds of the police. Two weeks later, on 2 February 1931, Wallace was charged with his wife's murder. He became very pale and replied: "What can I say to this charge, of which I am absolutely innocent?"

His trial began on 22 April, before Mr Justice Wright. The prosecution case was that Wallace had concocted an elaborate plan to murder his wife, and had phoned the café to make the appointment with Qualtrough on the evening before the murder. The endless and elaborate enquiries about Menlove Gardens East were intended to provide him with a perfect alibi; but Mrs Wallace was already lying dead in her sitting room when William Herbert Wallace left the house. In the closing speech for the crown, Mr E. G. Hemmerde made much of the "inherent improbabilities" in Wallace's story: that surely an insurance agent would not spend his evening on such a wild goose chase, that he would have hurried back home the moment he knew that a Menlove Gardens East did not exist. He also made much of Wallace's apparent calmness immediately after the discovery of the body, and mentioned in passing the possibility that Wallace had stripped naked and then put on his mackintosh, and battered his wife to death, before leaving the house to look for Qualtrough.

The judge's summing up was favourable to Wallace, and there was some surprise when, after only an hour, the jury returned a verdict of guilty. Wallace was shattered, he had been confident of acquittal. But he appealed against the verdict, and in the following month, the Court of Criminal Appeal quashed it, and Wallace was freed.

He was taken back at his old job. But most of his colleagues had doubts about his innocence. He was given a job in the office. He moved house to Meadowside Road in Bromsborough, a Liverpool suburb. And on 26 February 1933 — less than two years after his ordeal — he died in hospital of cancer of the liver. Ever since that date, writers on crime have disputed his guilt or innocence.

The main problem, of course, is that of motive. Wallace was a lifelong keeper of diaries, and his diaries make it clear that his married life was peaceful and serene. There was no suggestion of another woman, or that he was tired of his wife. His diaries after his trial continue to protest his innocence, with entries like: "Julia, Julia my dear, why were you taken from me?" The crime writer Nigel Morland, who examined the case at length in *Background to Murder* and who was convinced of Wallace's guilt, has to fall back on generalizations like: "The human heart is always a vast mystery."

Yseult Bridges, who also wrote about the case, became convinced of Wallace's guilt when she read a series of "ghosted" articles about his life which appeared in *John Bull* in 1932. There Wallace remarks that he had matched his brains against some of the greatest chess players in the world. Yseult Bridges comments that "he was never more than a third rate player in an obscure little club", and concludes that Wallace was a pathological liar. But another writer, Jonathan Goodman, looked more closely into the matter, and concludes (in *The Killing of Julia Wallace*) that Wallace was telling the truth after all; in the 1920s he *had* played in "simultaneous exhibition matches" against world-famous players like Capablanca — and been thoroughly beaten.

Kenneth Gunnell, a parliamentary candidate from Redruth, Cornwall, independently discovered that Wallace was telling the truth about his chess opponents, and so began to study the case in detail. He made one odd discovery. Amy Wallace, the wife of Wallace's elder brother Joseph, was a tough and dominant lady, and Gunnell found out that in Malaya — where she had lived in the 1920s — Amy had been a member of a flagellation sect, and indulged in beating black boys. He noted that after his acquittal, Wallace sometimes acted like a man with something on his mind — not murder, perhaps, but some guilty secret. Could it be that Amy Wallace was Herbert Wallace's mistress, and that *she* murdered Julia? Mr Gunnell even speculated that the murder weapon was the metal handle of a riding whip. Unfortunately, Mr Gunnell's stimulating theory remained unpublished. Yet when I read the typescript of his book, I found myself ultimately unconvinced. Although my view of Wallace was rather negative — he seemed to me a cold-hearted egoist who had married Julia for her money (which he used to pay his debts), then treated her purely as a piece of domestic furniture — it seemed clear that he was simply not the type to indulge in affairs with highly dominant women; Amy Wallace probably terrified him.

In 1960 I collaborated with Patricia Pitman on *An Encyclopaedia of Murder*. Mrs Pitman was convinced of Wallace's guilt, I — in spite of misgivings about his character — of his innocence. He simply had no reason to kill Julia. Two or three years later, she surprised me by telling me that she was now convinced of Wallace's innocence. It seemed that she had been talking to one of Britain's leading crime experts, J. H. H. Gaute, a director of Harraps publishers, and he had told her the real identity of the murderer. I hastened to contact Joe Gaute, with whom I had had much friendly correspondence about murder. It was from him that I first heard the name of the man he was certain was the killer of Julia Wallace: Gordon Parry. Wallace himself, it seemed, had believed that Parry murdered his wife, and after his retirement had made a public statement to the effect that he had had an alarm button installed inside his front door.

After the murder, Wallace had been asked by the police what callers might have been admitted to the house by his wife; he named fifteen people (including his sister-in-law Amy). Asked if he suspected any of them Wallace hesitated, then admitted that he was suspicious of a young man named Gordon Parry. This man had called at his house on business, and was trusted by Julia. But he had a criminal record. And he knew where Wallace kept his collection money. At the time of the murder, Parry was heavily in debt. Questioned by the police, Parry alleged that he had been with "friends" on the evening of the murder, and the friends corroborated this; however, two years later, Parry admitted that it had been "a mistake".

Crime writer Jonathan Goodman, who was writing a book on the Wallace case, tracked down Parry's father through the Liverpool town clerk, and from him obtained Gordon Parry's address in Camberwell, South London. Together with another crime expert, Richard Whittington-Egan, Goodman went to call on him.

Parry, a powerfully built little man with sleeked-back grey hair and a military moustache, received them with the "bogus bonhomie of a car salesman", and talked to them on his doorstep. They decided that "his manner masks . . . considerable firmness, even ruthlessness. He would be a nasty man to cross." Parry hinted that he could reveal much about Wallace, and described him as "a very strange man" and "sexually odd". He seemed to know what had become of everybody involved in the case, as if he had been carefully following its aftermath over the years. And when he finally dismissed Goodman and Whittington-Egan, they both had the feeling that he was thinking that he had fooled better people than they were . . . In his book *The Killing of Julia Wallace*, Goodman refers to Parry as "Mr X", and it is fairly clear that he regards him as the chief suspect.

In 1980, a news editor in Liverpool's Radio City, Roger Dilkes, became interested in the Wallace case, and started researching it for a programme. He contacted Jonathan Goodman, who at first was understandably cagey about revealing Parry's identity, in case he found himself involved in a libel suit. But through Wallace's solicitor, Hector Munro, Dilkes tracked down Parry's identity. At the time of the murder, Parry was twenty-two. The son of well-to-parents, he had worked for the Prudential for a while, but had failed to pay in various premiums he had received – his parents had paid the money. Parry had been charged at various times with theft, embezzlement and indecent assault – at his trial a medical expert had described him as "a sexual pervert".

Dilkes persisted, but when he finally tracked down Parry to North Wales, he discovered that he had died a few weeks before, in April 1980. Nevertheless, he continued with his investigation. Who were the "friends" who had given Parry his alibi for the night of the murder? The answer that emerged was that it was not friends but *a* friend – a Miss Lily Lloyd, to whom Parry was engaged. And from Jonathan Goodman he learned that when Parry had jilted her two years later, Miss Lloyd had gone to Wallace's solicitor and offered to swear an *affidavit* saying that the alibi she had given Parry for the night of the crime was untrue. Dilkes then managed to track down Miss Lloyd, who had played a piano in a cinema in the 1930s. If the police had taken the trouble to check *her* alibi, they would have learned that she could not have been with Parry at the time of the murder – she was working in the cinema.

Finally, Dilkes uncovered the clinching piece of evidence. At the time of the murder, a young garage mechanic named John Parkes had been working near Parry's home. He knew

Parry as a "wide boy" — in fact, had been to school with him. On the night of the murder, Parry had called at the garage in an agitated state, and washed down his car with a high pressure hose. Parkes saw a glove in the car, and pulled it out to prevent it getting wet. It was soaked with wet blood.

Dilkes had finally tracked down the murderer of Julia Wallace, but half a century too late.

The Harry Whitecliffe Mystery

According to a book published in France in 1978, one of England's most extraordinary mass murderers committed suicide in a Berlin jail in the middle of the jazz era. His name was Harry Whitecliffe, and he murdered at least forty women. Then why is his name not more widely known — at least to students of crime? Because when he was arrested he was masquerading under the name Lovach Blume, and his suicide concealed his true identity from the authorities.

The full story can be found in a volume called *Nouvelles Histoires Magiques — New Tales of Magic —* by Louis Pauwels and Guy Breton, published by Editions J"ai Lu. In spite of the title — which sounds like fiction — it is in fact a series of studies in the paranormal and bizarre; there are chapters on Nostradamus, Rasputin and Eusapia Palladino, and accounts of such well-known mysteries as the devil's footprints in Devon.

According to the chapter "The Two Faces of Harry Whitecliffe", there appeared in London in the early Twenties a collection of essays so promising that it sold out in a few days; it consisted of a series of marvellous pastiches of Oscar Wilde. But its author, Harry Whitecliffe, apparently preferred to shun publicity; he remained obstinately hidden.

Would-be interviewers returned empty-handed. Then, just as people were beginning to suggest that Whitecliffe was a pseudonym for some well-known writer — Bernard Shaw, perhaps, or the young T. S. Eliot — Whitecliffe finally consented to appear. He was a handsome young man of twenty-three, likeable, eccentric and fond of sport. He was also generous; he was said to have ended one convivial evening by casually giving a pretty female beggar £500. He professed to adore flowers, but only provided their stems were not more than twenty centimetres long. He was the kind of person the English love, and was soon a celebrity.

Meanwhile he continued to write: essays, poetry and plays. One of his comedies, *Similia*, had four hundred consecutive performances in London before touring England. It made him a fortune, which he quickly scattered among his friends. By the beginning of 1923, he was one of the "kings of London society".

Then, in September of that year, he vanished. He sold all his possessions, and gave his publisher carte blanche to handle his work. But before the end of the year he reappeared in Dresden. The theatre then presented *Similia* with enormous success, the author himself translating it from English into German. It went on to appear in many theatres along the Rhine. He founded a press for publishing modern poetry, and works on modern painting — Dorian Verlag — whose editions are now worth a fortune.

But he was still something of a man of mystery. Every morning he galloped along the banks of the river Elbe until nine o'clock; at ten he went to his office, eating lunch there. At six in the evening, he went to art exhibitions or literary salons, and met friends. At nine, he returned home and no one knew what he did for the rest of the evening. And no one liked to ask him.

One reason for this regular life was that he was in love — the girl was called Wally von Hammerstein, daughter of aristocratic parents, who were favourably impressed with the young writer. Their engagement was to be announced on 4 October 1924.

But on the previous day Whitecliffe disappeared again. He failed to arrive at his office, and vanished from his flat. The frantic Wally searched Dresden, without success. The police were alerted — discreetly — and pursued diligent inquiries. Their theory was that he had committed suicide. Wally believed he had either met with an accident or been the victim of a crime — he often carried large sums of money. As the weeks dragged by her desperation turned to misery; she talked about entering a convent.

Then she received a letter. It had been found in the cell of a condemned man who had committed suicide in Berlin — he had succeeded in opening his veins with the buckle of his belt. The inscription on the envelope said: "I beg you, monsieur le procureur of the Reich, to forward this letter to its destination without opening it." It was signed: Lovach Blume.

Blume was apparently one of the most horrible of murderers, worse than Jack the Ripper or Peter Kürten, the Düsseldorf sadist. He had admitted to the court that tried him: "Every ten days I have to kill. I am driven by an irresistible urge, so that until I have killed, I suffer atrociously. But as I disembowel my victims I feel an indescribable pleasure." Asked about his past, he declared: "I am a corpse. Why bother about the past of a corpse?"

Blume's victims were prostitutes and homeless girls picked up on the Berlin streets. He would take them to a hotel, and kill them as soon as they were undressed. Then, with a knife like a Malaysian "kris", with an ivory handle, he would perform horrible mutilations, so awful that even doctors found the sight unbearable. These murders continued over a period of six months, during which the slum quarters of Berlin lived in fear.

Blume was finally arrested by accident, in September 1924. The police thought he was engaged in drug trafficking, and knocked on the door of a hotel room minutes after Blume had entered with a prostitute. Blume had just committed his thirty-first murder in Berlin; he was standing naked by the window, and the woman's body lay at his feet.

He made no resistance, and admitted freely to his crimes — he could only recall twenty-seven. He declared that he had no fear of death — particularly the way executions were performed in Germany (by decapitation), which he greatly preferred to the English custom of hanging.

This was the man who had committed suicide in his prison cell, and who addressed a long letter to his fiancée, Wally von Hammerstein. He told her that he was certain the devil existed, because he had met him. He was, he explained, a kind of Jekyll-and-Hyde, an intelligent, talented man who suddenly became cruel and bloodthirsty. He thought of himself as being like victims of demoniacal possession. He had left London after committing nine murders, when he suspected that Scotland Yard was on his trail. His love for Wally was genuine, he told her, and had caused him to "die a little". He had hoped once that she might be able to save him from his demons, but it had proved a vain hope.

Wally fainted as she read the letter. And in 1925 she entered a nunnery and took the name Marie de Douleurs. There she prays for the salvation of a tortured soul. . . .

This is the story, as told by Louis Pauwels — a writer who became famous for his collaboration with Jacques Bergier on a book called *The Morning of the Magicians*. Critics pointed out that that book was full of factual errors, and a number of these can also be found in his article on Whitecliffe. For example, if the date of Blume's arrest is correct — 25 September 1924 — then it took place before Whitecliffe vanished from Dresden, on 3 October 1924 . . . But this, presumably, is a slip of the pen.

But who was Harry Whitecliffe? According to Pauwels, he told the Berlin court that his father was German, his mother Danish, and that he was brought up in Australia by an uncle who was a butcher. His uncle lived in Sydney. But in a "conversation" between Pauwels and his fellow-author at the end of one chapter, Pauwels states that Whitecliffe was the son of a great English family. But apart from the three magistrates who opened the suicide letter — ignoring Blume's last wishes — only Wally and her parents knew Whitecliffe's true identity. The judges are dead, so are Wally's parents. Wally is a seventy-five-year-old nun who until now has never told anyone of this drama of her youth. We are left to assume that she has now told the story to Pauwels.

This extraordinary tale aroused the curiosity of a well-known French authoress, Françoise d''Eaubonne, who felt that Whitecliffe deserved a book to himself. But her letters to the two authors — Pauwels and Breton — went unanswered. She therefore contacted the British Society of Theatre Research, and so entered into a correspondence with the theatre historian John Kennedy Melling. Melling had never heard of Whitecliffe, or of a play called *Similia*. He decided to begin his researches by contacting Scotland Yard, to ask whether they have any record of an unknown sex killer of the early 1920s. Their reply was negative; there was no series of Ripper-type murders of prostitutes in the early 1920s. He next applied to J. H. H. Gaute, the possessor of the largest crime library in the British Isles; Gaute could also find no trace of such a series of sex crimes in the 1920s. Theatrical reference books contained no mention of Harry Whitecliffe, or of his successful comedy *Similia*. It began to look — as incredible as it sounds — as if Pauwels had simply invented the whole story.

Thelma Holland, Oscar Wilde's daughter-in-law, could find no trace of a volume of parodies of Wilde among the comprehensive collection of her late husband, Vyvyan Holland. But she had a suggestion to make — to address inquiries to the Mitchell Library in Sydney. As an Australian, she felt it was probably Melling's best chance of tracking down Harry Whitecliffe.

Incredibly, this long shot brought positive results: not about Harry Whitecliffe, but about a German murderer called Blume — not Lovach, but Wilhelm Blume. The *Argus* newspaper for 8 August 1922 contained a story headed "Cultured Murderer", and sub-titled: "Literary Man's Series of Crimes". It was datelined Berlin, 7 August.

> Wilhelm Blume, a man of wide culture and considerable literary gifts, whose translations of English plays have been produced in Dresden with great success, has confessed to a series of cold-blooded murders, one of which was perpetrated at the Hotel Adlon, the best known Berlin hotel.

The most significant item in the newspaper report is that Blume had founded a publishing house called Dorian Press (Verlag) in Dresden. This is obviously the same Blume who — according to Pauwels — committed suicide in Berlin.

But Wilhelm Blume was not a sex killer. His victims had been postmen, and the motive had been robbery. In Germany postal orders were paid to consignees in their own homes, so postmen often carried fairly large sums of money. Blume had sent himself postal orders, then killed the postmen and robbed them — the exact number is not stated in the *Argus* article. The first time he did this he was interrupted by his landlady while he was strangling the postman with a noose; and he cut her throat. Then he moved on to Dresden, where in due course he attempted to rob another postman. Armed with two revolvers, he waited for the postman in the porch of a house. But the tenant of the house arrived so promptly that he had to flee, shooting one of the policemen. Then his revolvers both misfired, and he was caught. Apparently he attempted to commit suicide in prison, but failed. He confessed — as the *Argus* states — to several murders, and was presumably executed later in 1922 (although the *Argus* carries no further record).

It seems plain, then, that the question "Who was Harry Whitecliffe?" should be reworded "Who was Wilhelm Blume?" For Blume and Whitecliffe were obviously the same person.

From the information we possess, we can make a tentative reconstruction of the story of Blume–Whitecliffe. He sounds like a typical example of a certain type of killer who is also a confidence man — other examples are Landru, Petiot, the "acid bath murderer" Haigh, and the sex killer Neville Heath. It is an essential part of such a man's personality that he is a fantasist, and that he likes to pose as a success, and to talk casually about past triumphs. (Neville Heath called himself "Group Captain Rupert Brooke".) They usually start off as petty swindlers, then gradually become more ambitious and graduate to murder. This is what Blume seems to have done. In the chaos of postwar Berlin he made a quick fortune by murdering and robbing postmen. Perhaps his last coup made him a fortune beyond his expectations, or perhaps the Berlin postal authorities were now on the alert for the killer. Blume decided it was time to make an attempt to live a respectable life, and to put his literary fantasies into operation. He moved to Dresden, calling himself Harry Whitecliffe, and set up Dorian Verlag. He became a successful translator of English plays, and may have helped to finance their production in Dresden and in theatres along the Rhine. Since he was posing as an upper class Englishman, and must have occasionally run into other Englishmen in Dresden, we may assume that his English was perfect, and that his story of being brought up in Australia was probably true. Since he also spoke perfect German, it is also a fair assumption that he was, as he told the court, the son of a German father and a Danish mother.

He fell in love with an upper class girl, and told her a romantic story that is typical of the inveterate daydreamer:

that he was the son of a "great English family", that he had become an overnight literary success in London as a result of his pastiches of Oscar Wilde, but had at first preferred to shun the limelight (this is the true Walter Mitty touch) until increasing success made this impossible. His wealth is the result of a successful play, *Similia*. (The similarity of the title to *Salome* is obvious, and we may infer that Blume was an ardent admirer of Wilde.) But in order to avoid too much publicity — after all, victims of previous swindles might expose him — he lives the quiet, regular life of a crook in hiding.

And just as all seems to be going so well — just as success, respectability, a happy marriage, seem so close — he once again runs out of money. There is only one solution: a brief return to a life of crime. One or two robberies of postmen can replenish his bank account and secure his future . . . But this time it goes disastrously wrong. Harry Whitecliffe is exposed as the swindler and murderer Wilhelm Blume. He makes no attempt to deny it, and confesses to his previous murders; his world has now collapsed in ruins. He is sent back to Berlin, where the murders were committed, and he attempts suicide in his cell. Soon after, he dies by the guillotine. And in Dresden the true story of Wilhelm Blume is soon embroidered into a horrifying tale of a Jekyll-and-Hyde mass murderer, whose early career in London is confused with Jack the Ripper. . . .

Do any records of Wilhelm Blume still exist? It seems doubtful — the fire-bombing of Dresden destroyed most of the civic records, and the people who knew him more than sixty years ago must now all be dead. Yet Pauwels has obviously come across some garbled and wildly inaccurate account of Blume's career as Harry Whitecliffe. It would be interesting to know where he obtained his information; but neither Françoise d'"Eaubonne nor John Kennedy Melling have been successful in persuading him to answer letters.

Chapter Five

Hollywood Scandals

O ne of the first great successes to come out of the west coast village called Hollywood was The Life of an American Fireman (made in 1902 — The Great Train Robbery came the following year). The excited patrons saw a house on fire, a man being rescued from an upstairs window, then a woman and a child, coughing and staggering as they are overcome with smoke. The firemen dash through the streets on their horse-drawn wagons. As the mother and child collapse, unconscious, a fireman bursts in through the door. He carries the unconscious mother to a ladder that appears at the window; she wakes and begs him to save her baby. He carries her down, then goes back into the burning building, and gets the child. Mother and child are united as the house blazes. There wasn't a dry eye in the cinema. It had only lasted a few minutes, but people felt as if they'd been through a crisis together; they smiled through their tears at their next door neighbour. What a noble, interesting thing life is, after all! And the cinema could suddenly bring it home to you . . . It deserves to be classified with the novel as one of the greatest imaginative advances in human history.

Then there was Chaplin, the comic but game little tramp, always in trouble, always fighting against the odds, always looking shyly and adoringly at the pretty girl in the spring dress — and often getting her in the end. People could certainly identify with him. Chaplin records his amazement when he left Hollywood, where he'd been churning out two-reelers for years, to visit England and other towns in the United States, to realize that he was world famous. It wasn't just because Chaplin was a great performer. It was because he came from Hollywood — a word that was acquiring a dubious quality called "glamour". Hollywood was a magic land, a kind of fairyland on earth.

Many of its inhabitants held the same view, though for different reasons. It was soon clear that there was as much money in movies as in oil. Even the most successful actors and comedians could only play in one theatre at a time; but a movie could be shown in a hundred vaudeville theatres and Nickelodeons all over the country. One of the earliest successes, Rescued by Rover (made in England), cost seven pounds thirteen shillings and ninepence to produce (in 1905). The prints — 400 of them — sold for a little over £10 each, so the producer, Hepworth, multiplied his investment by five hundred or so. The Dream of a Rarebit Fiend cost $350 to make, and made $30,000. When the full length "drama" came in, around 1915, a movie might cost $50,000 and make a million. Producers found themselves unimaginably rich, rich on the scale of an eastern potentate. Their way of spending their money was to shower it on stars, directors and sets. In 1905, $10 a week was regarded as a reasonable wage for an actor; by 1920, a star could receive $100,000 for a movie that took ten weeks to make. Hollywood had the glamour of immense riches.

It was the Arbuckle case of 1921 that shocked the general public into realizing that many of its celluloid heroines and saints were nymphomaniacs and sinners. The studios had always done their best to hush up divorces and similar scandals. But now the jolly, fat-boy of the screen, who looked so completely amiable (as, indeed, he was), was suddenly associated with a rape ending in death. The lid was off Hollywood, and the stench was like a graveyard. In her best known photograph, Virginia Rappe looked so sweet and wholesome, the kind of girl every decent American boy wanted to marry. The thought of the manner of her death aroused a kind of morbid fascination; the grinning Fatty Arbuckle became a real life Dracula or Jack the Ripper. He was acquitted, and the jury foreman at his last trial said: "We feel a great injustice has been done him." Arbuckle chortled with delight; the studio bosses announced more Arbuckle pictures. They had simply failed to understand that once an idol has been *de-glamorized, there can be no come-back. Possibly Arbuckle might have made a new career as an actor in horror movies, to fit his new image; but no one thought of that. He died of a heart attack in 1933, a tired and disappointed man.*

The Murder of William Desmond Taylor

And in the year after the Arbuckle scandal, while the fat clown was still on trial, another scandal struck Hollywood like an earth tremor. The victim was the suave, handsome British film director William Desmond Taylor. Taylor was a cultured man who was enthusiastic about the works of Freud. No doubt he found himself in agreement with Freud's thesis that the libido is the basic animal drive, for he himself had an insatiable sexual appetite. And as the $100,000 a year chief-director of Lasky Studios (later Paramount), he had no difficulty in keeping himself supplied with a stream of young girls, all of whom wanted to marry him. Taylor had no intention of marrying anyone for a long time; he was enjoying life too much. Then, on 21 February 1922, it came to a sudden end. His valet, Peavy, returning to Taylor's expensive Westlake Park home at 7.30 in the morning, found his master lying on his back, quite dead. The death was assumed to be natural until Taylor was turned over, and two bullet holes were seen. The police searching the house found evidence of Taylor's incredible love-life, including a note from a popular star of the day, Mary Miles Minter — a Chaplin leading lady — which read "Dearest, I love you, I love you, I love you" with a whole row of kisses. At Taylor's funeral, she kissed the corpse on the lips. Like Arbuckle, she was unaware of the attitude of the outside world to the idols who inhabited their dream paradise. They were supposed to live up to their screen image of purity and innocence. Miss Minter's career came

Hollywood began as a ranch near the small town of Los Angeles in 1886. In 1913, a New York film company run by two men named Schmuel Gelbfisz and Jesse Lasky sent their new employee Cecil B. DeMille to Flagstaff, Arizona, looking for a place to make westerns. Flagstaff was too flat, so he got back on the train and went on to Los Angeles, where he rented a barn on the Hollywood ranch, and made a smash hit called *The Squaw Man*.

Schmel Gelbfisz was already calling himself Samuel Goldfish, but he then decided on a further change — to Samuel Goldwyn. Under that name he is known as the author of some famous remarks, such as "Include me out", and "My film *Hans Christian Andersen* is full of charmth and warmth". He always referred to the classic film made by his own studio as *Withering Heights*. When told that he could not make *The Well of Loneliness* because it was about lesbians, he said, "Ok, make 'em Austrians."

to an end with the scandal. So did that of Mabel Normand, a comedienne who, next to Mary Pickford, was Hollywood's most popular actress. Miss Normand had spent an hour or so with Taylor the evening before his death, although she had left early. She claimed to be his fiancée. But police discovered that the angelic-looking Miss Normand had been experimenting with drugs, and that Taylor had been doing his best to track down whoever was supplying her.

In fact, the aftermath of Taylor's death was almost worse than the murder itself. It emerged that Miss Minter was not twenty, as she was supposed to be, but thirty. Peavy, the valet, was very obviously homosexual, and for a while, this seemed to supply a possible motive for the crime. For Taylor's previous valet, a man named Sands, had been forging cheques in Taylor's name while his master was in Europe, and smashing his cars. Yet when he returned, Taylor only fired him. Since then, Taylor had been burgled twice. Was it possible that Sands was Taylor's lover, and had killed him out of jealousy or revenge? This notion was exploded when it was revealed that "Sands" was actually Taylor's disreputable brother Denis, who had come to America with him years before. Denis was never located.

In 1967, the famous director King Vidor decided to turn the Taylor mystery into a film. What he learned about the power of the studios and the corruption of the Los Angeles police department shocked him. To begin with, Adolph Zukor and other executives of Famous Players Lasky had descended on Taylor's house immediately after the murder and destroyed a quantity of letters and papers. But according to information leaked to the press, the police had no difficulty finding out that Taylor had been having affairs with half the celebrated beauties of Hollywood. They also found quantities of silk knickers in Taylor's bedroom — souvenirs, apparently, of his many conquests, as well as pornographic photographs showing Taylor in the act of lovemaking with various ladies, and a pink silk nightie monogrammed MMM.

Mary Miles Minter and Mabel Normand were naturally among the suspects. So was Mary's mother, Charlotte Shelby, a tough Hollywood Mom who may have been in love with Taylor herself. But she, apparently, had a good alibi.

When Vidor's biographer, Sidney Kirkpatrick, began gathering material for his book, he discovered that a whole year seemed to be missing from his papers: 1967. When he found the missing papers in a locked strongbox in the garage, he discovered that they concerned Vidor's inves-

tigations of the Taylor case. And when he read them, he
saw why Vidor had decided to abandon the whole project.

It seemed that Vidor had soon discovered that Taylor
was not what he pretended to be; the evidence indicated
that the insatiable Don Juan was, in fact, a bisexual, with a
distinct preference for men, and (quite possibly) for young
boys, who were procured by his valet. And at least one
Hollywood journalist was able to tell Vidor authoritatively
that the killer was the mother of Mary Miles Minter, the
ambitious and ruthless Charlotte Shelby who, like everyone
else, was unaware of Taylor's true sexual inclinations.
Charlotte was not only fixated on Taylor; she was also
quite determined that her daughter — who was also her meal
ticket — should not get involved with any man. It seems that
on the evening in question, Mary was having a tête-a-tête
with Taylor when Mabel Normand turned up; so Mary fled
into hiding. Her mother became increasingly irritable, and
finally went looking for her with a pistol. She saw Mabel
Normand emerge from Taylor's house, then peered in
through the window and saw her daughter coming out
of hiding. This was too much and she stalked in and shot the
dastardly seducer — in the back, having made him raise his
arms.

So what about all the stories of underwear and pornographic pictures? These, apparently, were the work of the
film studio, which promptly went into action to throw up a
heavy smoke screen. Hollywood had enough scandals —
Fatty Arbuckle had just been arrested — and they had no
intention of this one reaching court. So the press was fed
with scandalous stories about silk nighties. The careers of
Mary Miles Minter and Mabel Normand were ruined, but
the wicked Charlotte lived on and prospered.

According to Kirkpatrick, Vidor decided to give up the
film because he didn't want to taint the lives of the stars
concerned. He may also have been worried about libel. But
surely the true answer is that even in 1967, a film about a

Mabel Normand's career experienced a setback as a result of the William Desmond Taylor affair, but it was wrecked by a further scandal in 1924. She was visiting Chaplin's leading lady Edna Purviance and her oilman lover Cortland S. Dines; all got very drunk. When Edna's chauffeur came to pick her up, he and Dines got into an argument and the chauffeur shot Dines, slightly wounding him. (The chauffeur was obviously her lover.) At a hearing, it was revealed that the chauffeur was a convicted criminal and a drug addict. This, combined with the fact that the women were drunk on bootleg liquor (1924 was the middle of the Prohibition) and that everyone was rumoured to be naked, was the final nail in the coffin of Mabel's career.

Don Juan who turned out to be a homosexual paedophile was just not good Hollywood material. That particular can of worms was just a little too putrid.

The Jean Harlow Mystery

In the early Thirties, some Hollywood producers decided they might as well cash in on the bad reputation of the movie capital. So while some studios were making fortunes with films like *Little Women* and *Rebecca of Sunnybrook Farm*, others introduced a new frankness to the screen. Mae West's line "Come up, see me sometime" became the great catch phrase of the day. Middle-aged men and women chuckled appreciatively when she sang:

"I Like a Man Who Takes His Time". And the latest screen idol was a blonde newcomer called Harlean Carpenter, who chose the screen name Jean Harlow. Harlow replaced Clara Bow, the "It" girl, in the public's estimation; Clara Bow lost her reputation in 1930, when her ex-secretary testified in court that she was virtually a nymphomaniac, spending her large income on good-looking gigolos. Yet even Harlow — whose screen personality was nearly as uninhibited as Mae West's — felt the chilly breath of scandal when her husband, the director and movie-supervisor Paul Bern, was found shot dead under mysterious circumstances in September 1932. Amusingly enough, what alarmed the studios was not that the public might feel Harlow was as wicked as her screen parts, but that she might arouse pity — and contempt. She had been married to Bern — who was regarded as a Hollywood "genius" — for only two months, and reports said they were ideally happy. But police investigation revealed that, for many years before marrying Harlow, Bern had lived with another lovely blonde, Dorothy Millette. After a nervous breakdown, Dorothy had spent some time in a mental home, then continued to live in the Algonquin Hotel in New York, at Bern's expense. She killed herself the day after Paul's death — she was in San Francisco at the time. Was it she who had killed Bern? Bern was naked when he was found, and a woman's wet swimsuit had been found beside the swimming pool. Hollywood was afraid that Harlow might arouse pity as a woman who could not keep her husband — and that would ruin her screen image just as surely as the Taylor scandal had ruined Mabel Normand's.

There were whispers of an even more embarrassing nature. Jean Harlow told friends, in the strictest confidence, that Bern was impotent. On the night before his death, he had come into her bedroom wearing a huge artificial phallus, and had pranced around the room with it

Jean Harlow with her husband, film director Hal Rosson.

on, until the two of them, shrieking with laughter, tore it to pieces with scissors and flushed it down the lavatory.

In 1960, the Hollywood screenwriter Ben Hecht wrote an article in *Playboy* claiming that Bern *had* been murdered by another woman, probably Dorothy Millette. The studio had forged the suicide note. Yet in retrospect, Hecht's version seems unlikely. Why did Dorothy Millette have a nervous breakdown in the first place — was it because Bern was impotent? Why did she and Bern never live together again, although they remained fond of one another? (The tone of the letters exchanged between them makes it unlikely that she would kill him.) The note itself sounds too authentic to be a forgery. It said: "Unfortunately, this is the only way to make good the frightful wrong I have done you and to wipe out my abject humiliation. I love you"; a postscript added, "You understand last night was only a comedy". That has the ring of authenticity, and it fits the story of impotence and the dildo episode. The fact that Bern was naked when he was shot also suggests self-humiliation.

Four years later, in 1936, Jean Harlow also died, of a gall bladder infection. She was twenty-six. There were many American matrons who felt it was divine justice.

The Death of Thelma Todd

In 1935, another Hollywood tragedy ended in murder — although it is still officially listed as suicide. Thelma Todd became Miss Massachusetts at the age of sixteen, and shortly thereafter, she threw up a job as a teacher to go to Hollywood. In 1926, when she was twenty-one, she appeared with fifteen other promising "starlets" in a film called *Fascinating Youth*, and her career was launched. Her real talent proved to be in comedy, and the beautiful and statuesque blonde appeared with Laurel and Hardy and the

Marx Brothers. ("Madame, you're making history. Madame, you're making me, I wish you'd keep your hands to yourself.") She was a kind, good-natured, popular girl, with an odd touch of sadness, a feeling that life — or perhaps just her life — was unreal. In 1932 — when she was twenty-seven — she married an agent named Di Cicco, but two years later they were divorced. She had already decided to retire from films and go into the restaurant business in 1935 when Stanley Lupino and his daughter Ida decided to give a party for her. Di Cicco came to the restaurant and there was a quarrel. In the early hours of a Sunday morning in December 1935, she was driven to her home in Santa Monica. More than twenty-four hours later, she was found dead in her car, in the garage above the beach restaurant she owned. There was blood on her face, and she still wore the party clothes. She had died of carbon monoxide poisoning. The odd thing was that her evening slippers showed no sign of the wear they would have received climbing the rough concrete stairs — 270 of them — from the beach to the garage. All the evidence pointed to murder — particularly when it was discovered that she had been alive on the Sunday after the party, and had been seen in a car with a dark, foreign-looking man. It looked very much as if he had driven into the garage with her, knocked her unconscious, then turned on the exhaust and left her.

Again, the movie moguls went into a frantic scramble of panic. A scandal of this sort was the last thing the studio wanted. The police suddenly announced that, in spite of the blood on her face, they were treating Thelma Todd's death as a case of suicide. Even when they received a telegram from Ogden, Utah, saying that Thelma Todd's killer was in a hotel there, they did nothing about it. The case has remained as mysterious as when it happened.

By 1968, the golden days of Hollywood were only a distant memory, and a death that occurred in a Spanish-style hilltop home above Laurel Canyon may be regarded as a sad postscript to the history of the great years. Ramon Navarro, the handsome star of *Ben Hur* and *The Prisoner of Zenda*, was found, naked and beaten to death, on his bed, his hands tied behind him. The house was ransacked. Navarro's telephone bill revealed that a long call had been made to Chicago on 30 October, the evening of his death. It was easy to discover that the call had been made by a young man named Tom Ferguson. The police arrested Tom and his brother Paul, a male prostitute. When they discovered that seventy-year-old Navarro, the idol of American women, had been homosexual, they had solved the case. The Ferguson brothers admitted going to Navarro's house — at his request — and then tying him up and beating him to make him reveal the whereabouts of money. He died from swallowing blood. The robbery netted the brothers about $45. Both brothers received life imprisonment.

The Mystery Death of Marilyn Monroe

But by far the most famous of all Hollywood scandal stories is the mystery surrounding the death of Marilyn Monroe.

The life of Hollywood's most famous "sex symbol" had been a tale of hardship and misfortune. Norma Jeane Baker (or Jean, as she sometimes spelt it) was born in Los Angeles in 1926, the illegitimate daughter of Gladys Pearl Baker (née Monroe), a film cutter at the Columbia and RKO studios, and a fellow lodger called C. Stanley Gifford. There was a history of mental instability and suicide in Gladys's family. For most of Norma Jean's childhood, her mother was confined in mental institutions, and from the age of five, the child spent most of her life in foster homes — no less than twelve of them. At the age of seven her mother had her back home to live, but then had a nervous breakdown and was hospitalized yet again. At the age of eight (other biographical sources say eleven) she was persuaded to remove her dress by a gentlemanly old boarder who caressed her genitals; finally, troubled by his excitement, she put her clothes back on and went to tell her foster mother, who told her angrily to shut up. But she later admitted to a lover that the experience had not been traumatic — in fact, that she had found it oddly pleasant.

At sixteen, she married a twenty-one-year-old aircraft-worker, Jim Dougherty, mainly to gain her independence, but they had little in common; a year later, she made her first suicide attempt. In the same year she became a paint sprayer in a defence plant and was "discovered" by an army photographer; her "pin-ups" achieved great success among GIs, and the army medical corps voted her the girl they would most like to examine. During this period, she later confessed to Ted Jordan, an actor who became her lover, she often went out to bars, became acquainted with men, and allowed them to make love to her. It may be that her earlier sexual encounter with the boarder had established a pattern — the recognition that she could give men pleasure and excite their tenderness by removing her dress. She always seems to have been singularly frank about sex, describing it uninhibitedly in four-letter words.

By 1946 she had been to a charm school and become a successful model; soon afterwards she was signed on by 20th Century Fox at $125 a week, and her name changed to Marilyn Monroe.

The two years she spent as a Fox starlet were not a success; after two brief appearances she was dropped. Columbia signed her up, and she received good reviews playing the lead in a low budget musical, *Ladies of the Chorus*. But Columbia also allowed her contract to expire. While unemployed she posed for a nude calendar photograph, for which she was paid $50; it went on to make three quarters of a million dollars for the calendar company.

Marilyn Monroe.

Unsolved Crimes

In the 1950s, she returned to Fox, and although she always played the same dumb blonde, her popularity increased slowly but surely. She herself was frank about the extent to which her success was due to granting her sexual favours to directors and agents: she commented: "I spent a lot of time on my knees." But her sexual acquiescence was also the secret of her immense success on the screen: it was the combination of physical beauty and the hint of submissiveness, of availability, that made her every man's dream. It was also the basic cause of her downfall; every man wanted her, and her desire to please meant that she often said yes. The list of her lovers was immense, and one writer estimates that she had as many as fourteen abortions.

Her marriage to baseball star Joe Di Maggio in 1954 confirmed her status as Hollywood's latest "sex goddess". But he wanted a wife rather than a movie star, and they divorced only nine months later.

Deciding that she wanted to be a "real actress" she went to New York to study at the Actors Studio, where she met the playwright Arthur Miller. Back at Fox, she was now the most valuable property in Hollywood, and her salary reflected this. But she was also well known for her unpunctuality and unreliability. This was due mainly to her depressions, and their accompanying listlessness. Marriage to Arthur Miller in 1956 seemed to stabilize her, but after an affair with her co-star Yves Montand in 1960, they were divorced. After that she embarked on an affair with Frank Sinatra.

Miller had written a screenplay especially for her — *The Misfits*, a grim and depressing piece of work about drifters that contributed to the death of one of its male stars, Clark Gable, and which increased her tendency to depression. A month after the premiere she had a total breakdown and entered a psychiatric hospital. On the set of her final film, *Something's Got to Give*, her behaviour became increasingly erratic, until she was finally sacked.

No one, therefore, was greatly surprised when, on 5 August 1962, her housekeeper found her naked and lifeless body on her bed, apparently a victim of suicide (although there was no suicide note). The coroner's verdict was death by an overdose of barbiturates — Nembutal. Yet there were some odd discrepancies. Although there were huge quantities of barbiturates in her bloodstream and liver, there was no sign of it in her stomach — an impossibility unless she had injected it. But no sign of needle punctures was found at the autopsy, and there was no syringe in the room.

Persistent rumours began to circulate that her death was not suicide, but murder. It had been widely known among journalists that Marilyn had had an affair with President Kennedy — a notorious womanizer — but it was less well known that she had later had an affair with his brother Robert, the Attorney General. A detective named Fred Otash later revealed that he had bugged the telephone in Marilyn's home at the behest of Bobby Kennedy. Kennedy spoke openly to Marilyn about some rather dangerous secrets, such as his intention of having Fidel Castro assassinated. (Thirteen years later, it was revealed that President Kennedy had authorized the CIA to try and assassinate Castro.) Kennedy also told her that he intended to get "that son of a bitch Jimmy Hoffa" into jail no matter what it cost him — Hoffa was head of the Teamsters Union and a man with known links to organized crime. Marilyn kept notes of these conversations because Kennedy was sometimes irritated by her failure to remember things he had said to her.

According to a man named Bob Slatzer, who claimed that he and Marilyn had been briefly married in 1946, Marilyn had been hoping to marry Bobby Kennedy, who had promised to divorce his wife. But Bobby Kennedy was warned off such an idea by his brother, and he accordingly broke with her not long before her death. She was bitter, and felt she had been used; she tried to ring Kennedy in

Washington many times, without success. She hinted strongly to the actor Peter Lawford that she was pregnant with Bobby Kennedy's child. More dangerously, she told Slatzer that she was thinking of calling a press conference to "blow the lid off the whole damn thing". She repeated the same thing to Lawford, declaring that she had been "used . . . thrown from one man to another" (which obviously referred to the Kennedys) and that she was "going public with everything". Since Lawford was John Kennedy's brother-in-law, this was a sure way of getting her message through to the President.

On the weekend she died, Robert Kennedy travelled to San Francisco to address a law conference. In his Monroe biography *Goddess*, Anthony Summers argues convincingly that Robert Kennedy came over to see her that afternoon, to explain that their affair had come to an end. In fact, neighbours reported seeing Robert Kennedy arrive with another man carrying what looked like a doctor's bag. Kennedy himself is alleged to have testified in a secret deposition that he had been there, and that the doctor had given Marilyn an injection of a strong sedative to calm her nerves.

It later emerged that Marilyn's home had also been "bugged" by an electronics expert named Bernard Spindel, who was employed by Jimmy Hoffa. Spindel subsequently went to prison, and alleged that he had also bugged the home of Peter Lawford. Hoffa's intention was to get compromising material about Robert Kennedy. Kennedy found out about the tapes of his conversation with Marilyn, and offered Spindel $25,000 for them, which Spindel refused.

That some kind of "cover up" had happened became clear in the years following her death. Peter Lawford admitted that she had telephoned him – sounding tired and slurry – to say goodbye during that last evening, and that he had wanted to rush over to see she was all right. He was dissuaded because it would compromise him. What

A policeman guarding the home of Marilyn Monroe after she was found dead in bed.

seems clear is that before her death was announced, someone rushed to her house to remove compromising material, such as the red notebook recording Kennedy's conversations — most writers on the case believe this was done by CIA agents on the orders of Robert Kennedy. The housekeeper, Mrs Murray, told two conflicting stories about the time she found Marilyn's body — that it was at midnight, and that it was at 3.30 a.m.

Most of this evidence seems to suggest suicide — except for the absence of barbiturates in her stomach. Is it possible that she injected herself with the drug, and that the telltale syringe was removed by the "searchers"? This is unlikely, since she is known to have been a "pill popper" who never used a syringe. Another possibility emerges from remarks made by Lawford's ex-wife Deborah Gould; she claims she asked her husband how Marilyn died, and that he replied: "She took her last big enema." This suggests that she was sometimes in the habit of taking drugs anally — which has a far quicker effect than taking them orally, since the drugs enter the large intestine immediately.

But if Marilyn sometimes took drugs by enema, then it is also possible that she was killed by the same method. People to whom she talked on the afternoon of her death say she sounded slurred. A neighbour who sometimes lent her sleeping pills says she asked to borrow some that afternoon; but there had been pills in the house in the morning. If she had been "popping pills" all day, she may have lapsed into unconsciousness, and been vulnerable to attack.

If she *was* murdered, then the chief suspect is bound to be Bobby Kennedy himself. The private detective Fred Otash claims that Lawford burst into his office at 3 a.m., announcing that Marilyn Monroe was dead, and that Bobby Kennedy was there — adding that Kennedy and Marilyn had "got into a big fight that evening". Otash went on to allege that he was then hired by Lawford to

Asked if it was true that she had nothing on when the famous calendar photograph was taken, Marilyn Monroe replied: "I had the radio on."

go to Marilyn's home and remove any evidence of links with the Kennedys.

Norman Mailer, in his biography of Marilyn Monroe, denies that the Kennedys could have been implicated in her death, because it would have been stupid of them to risk everything. His theory is that disaffected members of the CIA, angry about the bungled assassination attempt on Castro, killed Marilyn to destroy the Kennedy Administration. They left the room looking as if she had committed suicide, but knew that the lack of barbiturates in her stomach would point to murder. The finger would then be pointed at the Kennedys.

Since Jimmy Hoffa knew of the existence of the compromising tapes, he also had a motive for killing Marilyn Monroe. Her death, and the subsequent revelation of her affairs with both Kennedy brothers, would trigger a scandal, and would probably prevent Kennedy from being re-elected in 1964. In fact, Spindel's home was raided in 1966, on the orders of the Manhattan District Attorney, Frank Hogan, and all his equipment seized. He believed that this was inspired by Robert Kennedy. And members of the DA's staff subsequently told a reporter that the tapes contained evidence that "Marilyn had been murdered" and that Bobby Kennedy was involved "if only as a catalyst causing someone else to do it". This "someone else" was presumably Jimmy Hoffa.

But if Marilyn Monroe was murdered in order to ruin the Kennedys, then why did the scandal never explode as planned? Was it because the cover-up by the Kennedys was too efficient? (It is known that Marilyn's phone records for August were illegally seized from the General Telephone Company, presumably to hide the number of calls she made to Washington in her last days.) Even so, it is hard to believe that the Kennedys' many underworld enemies would have failed to make use of compromising material.

Milo Speriglio, a private detective hired by Robert Slatzer, has stated unequivocally: "Marilyn Monroe was politically assassinated" — for the sake of the tapes of sessions with Robert Kennedy, and the red notebook containing his "secrets". Speriglio later changed his opinion and came to believe that she was killed at the behest of Mafia boss Sam Giancana, who wanted her dead because she knew of his involvement in the plot to kill Castro.

One man who may know more of the truth than most is Marilyn's doctor, Ralph Greenson, to whom she talked confidentially on the afternoon before her death. Greenson says he cannot reveal what she said, but that it leads him to believe that her death was not suicide. Pressed for more information, he said exasperatedly: "Listen . . . talk to Bobby Kennedy."

Most of those who might have been able to tell the truth about Marilyn Monroe's death died without revealing it: President Kennedy in 1963, Robert Kennedy in 1965, Jimmy Hoffa in 1975. (Hoffa simply vanished, and has never been found.) The final verdict must be that Marilyn Monroe *could* have committed suicide — she had reason to do so — but that much of the evidence points towards murder. On the other hand, if Lawford's remark that she used enemas to administer drugs is correct, then suicide remains the likeliest possibility after all.

The Black Dahlia

No account of Los Angeles murder mysteries would be complete without a mention of the most gruesome riddle of all: the death of aspiring actress Elizabeth Short. Known as the Black Dahlia because of her preference for black underwear, "Beth" had spent much of her short life (she was twenty-two when she was murdered) wandering aimlessly — from Massachusetts to Florida, from Florida to California, then Chicago, then California again. Like Marilyn Monroe, she spent her life seeking security and affection.

In January 1947, her body was found in a vacant lot in Los Angeles, severed in half at the waist; medical examination revealed that she had been suspended upside down and tortured to death over many hours — the body was covered with cigarette burns and small cuts. The letters "BD" had been cut into her thigh.

The killer sent the police some of her personal possessions — including her birth certificate and address book — together with a letter made up of words and letters clipped

During Elizabeth Short's early days in Hollywood, she visited a fortune teller on Hollywood Boulevard with a friend called Marjorie Graham.

Marjorie recalled later that Beth Short had been in high spirits before they went to the fortune teller, but that when they left the gypsy, she seemed 'saddened and uneasy'.

'Whatever that woman told her had disturbed Beth. She seemed to have other things on her mind the rest of the day and was depressed.'

Unsolved Crimes

from newspapers. The horror of the crime made it headline news, and in due course, the police received twenty-eight confessions, all of which proved to be false. Two films have been made about the case, and a novel that suggests that she was involved in sadistic pornographic movies. But although more confessions have continued to pour in down the years, the case remains unsolved.

Chapter Six

Other Unsolved Murders

*I*n *The Murderer's Who's Who by J. H. H. Gaute and Robin Odell, there is only one entry for Australia under the heading "Unsolved murders", compared to five for America and thirteen for Britain. That one Australian entry concerns a rather commonplace gangland murder which has achieved a certain classic status largely because of the bizarre name under which it is usually classified: the Shark Arm Murder.*

A death in Kenya, East Africa, in 1941, eclipsed even the war when the body of Lord Erroll was found murdered in a ditch. And in Britain, witchcraft involvement added to the mystery of who murdered Charles Walton. How did he come to have a pagan symbol cut into his neck and chest?

The Shark Arm Murder

*O*n the morning of 18 April 1935, two Sydney fishermen finally subdued a fourteen foot tiger shark. The beast had been thrashing at the end of the line for most of the night, desperate to disentangle itself. The bait had been set out the previous evening, and had soon attracted a small shark. This more suitable catch had itself then brought the attentions of a monster tiger shark. Soon only the head of the small shark remained and it was the interloper that struggled on the line.

The shark was put on display at the Coogee aquarium, where it proved to be a popular attraction. On 25 April – an

Unsolved Crimes

The only other Australian murder mystery to
find its way into anthologies of true crime
concerns the death of fourteen-year-old Shirley
Collins. Pretty but extremely shy, Shirley was
invited to her first party at Richmond,
Melbourne, on 12 September 1953. She failed to
arrive. Two days later, her naked body was
found at Mount Martha, thirty-eight miles from
Melbourne. Her head had been crushed by a
heavy stone, and broken beer bottles with
bloody fingerprints were found nearby. (They
failed to identify her attacker.) Yet there had
been no sexual assault. She must have been
taken there by car – yet the idea of a forcible
kidnapping had to be ruled out since the streets
were crowded that Saturday evening. The
boyfriend who had invited her to the party had
a perfect alibi – he had waited for her on the
station for an hour and a half, seen by many
porters, then gone to the party. The idea that
the extremely shy girl might accept a lift from a
stranger also had to be ruled out. The biggest
police operation in Melbourne's history failed to
unearth a single clue as to why a girl who set
out for Richmond would end up so far away,
stripped and battered to death.

Australian public holiday – people flocked to the aquarium
to see the new exhibit. Since being caught the shark's health
had deteriorated, requiring extra oxygen to be pumped into
the water. To the crowd the shark seemed tired and listless,
flicking itself up and down its small tank as if in a trance.
Suddenly, as the crowd watched, it spiralled round itself

three times, vomiting black, oily clouds into the water. As the foul mess cleared a human arm, trailing a length of rope tied around its wrist, floated to the surface.

When the police arrived they carefully filtered the rest of the shark's vomit for human body parts. The shark itself was killed and slit open, but nothing further was found. The least sinister explanation was the first to be considered: that the arm belonged to a suicide. Mysteriously the shark had failed to even semi-digest the arm. Indeed, it was in such good condition that police were able to scalpel off the fingerprints and check them against records. A good match was found, a man called James Smith.

Smith, variously described as a builder, an engineer, a road labourer and bookie, had a string of minor convictions. When the police contacted his wife they were told that he had disappeared on 8 April, saying that he was going fishing with a friend. Unfortunately he had neglected to name the friend. Mrs Smith identified the arm by a small tattoo just above the wrist, depicting two men boxing. She told police that her husband had committed suicide.

This conclusion was being reached at the same time by Dr Victor Coppelson, an expert on shark bites who had been called in to examine the severing wound on Smith's arm. It was obvious to Coppelson, due to the clean appearance of the wound, that the arm had been cut off with a knife, not bitten or torn off by a shark. Someone had prepared the tiger shark's meal.

He also solved the mystery of why the arm was undigested. The shark had been sent into shock by its long struggle against the line; its digestive system had shut down. Coppelson also revealed that the arm had reached the tiger shark third-hand. Severed by an unknown human, the arm had been originally eaten by the smaller shark. In eating it, the tiger shark had also unwittingly eaten the arm.

The police were now investigating a murder. They immediately set about dragging the bay for the remainder of Smith's body. Meanwhile inquiries had turned up the nature of Smith's last job: he had been hired to guard and run a powerful motor launch called "Pathfinder". This gave police an insight into a possible motive for the murder . . .

In the 1930s Sydney was a violent city. There was a large criminal underworld controlling the flow of refined opium from the East to America. Ships sailing directly from the Far East to America's West Coast were thoroughly searched by coastguards. However, with ships from Australia the authorities were more lax. Thus, at Sydney, motor launches would transfer the opium from Far Eastern to America-bound ships under the cover of night. Many men made fortunes on this contraband trade. These men would hire poor labourers to run their launches, promising a small sum if they were ever imprisoned. Competition was fierce, leading in effect to a gang-war situation. Rivals' boats were sunk, and murder of the hired help was common.

Taking the next logical step, police traced "Pathfinder" and tried to contact its owner. They discovered that "Pathfinder" had been sunk at the beginning of April. Its owner was a Mr Reginald Holmes, a boat-builder and launch-proprietor who, it was rumoured, was an important figure on the narcotics scene. When interviewed Holmes seemed agitated, distancing himself from the crime by claiming that both he and Smith had been blackmailed by a rival launch-proprietor, Patrick Brady, ever since the sinking of "Pathfinder". The basis of this alleged blackmail was never made public, but seems likely to have centred around opium dealing. It was to see Brady, Holmes claimed, that Smith had set out on 8 April.

From this point the police's investigation becomes a catalogue of misjudgement. They took the precaution of arresting Brady on a trumped-up bureaucratic charge to prevent his flight. Holmes, for no explicable reason, was left without any police supervision. It seems clear that the

Sydney police chronically underestimated the violence of its criminal element.

While searching Brady's beach-hut police noticed several mysterious absences. The mattress off the bed had gone, as had a tin trunk. Three mats and a coil of rope were missing from Brady's boat.

Police invited Sir Sydney Smith, the great forensic scientist, who was at the time attending a conference in the city, to suggest how the disposal of the body was achieved. He obliged with a neat and plausible model. The body had been dismembered on the mats and the mattress, and the resulting pieces stuffed into the trunk. The body could not be completely contained however and so the arm was tied to the trunk with rope and, with the bloody mats, thrown into the sea. The trunk sank to the bottom, but the arm worked loose, eventually to be eaten by the small shark.

Unfortunately the police would soon have more to explain. Soon after Brady's arrest a motor launch was seen to be zig-zagging at a dangerous speed all around the bay. Policemen who tried to flag the boat down had to swerve to avoid being rammed. A long chase requiring half a dozen police boats eventually cornered the launch. At the controls was Reginald Holmes, smelling strongly of alcohol and bleeding heavily from a bullet wound in his head. He claimed that as he left his home that morning, a gunman had tried to kill him. Holmes had succeeded in escaping by fleeing in his launch. He had tried to escape the police because he thought they were gunmen too.

Whether the police believed Holmes's story, or whether they accepted the altogether more likely explanation that they had stumbled upon a failed suicide attempt, they seem to have had a grievous lack of foresight. Either situation would necessitate police surveillance, Holmes was after all their key witness against Brady, who was their only suspect. During his stay in hospital Holmes told police that he was sure Brady had killed Smith. He said that Brady had told him as much, and warned him that if he told the police, Brady or his friends would kill him. Amazingly, after he was discharged from hospital Holmes received no police protection.

On the morning of the inquest Holmes was found dead in his car, shot through the chest and groin. Deprived of their only witness, police were dealt another blow when the coroner refused to accept Smith's arm as a token of his death. Without a body, murder is extremely difficult to prove. The Sydney police had no real evidence without Holmes; thus Brady was released. Two associates of Brady who were arrested for the murder of Holmes also walked free due to insufficient evidence.

Rumours persist that it was in fact Holmes who dismembered Jim Smith, afterwards paying Brady to take the prison sentence. All that is certain is that, through police incompetence, the case remains officially unsolved.

The Death of Lord Erroll

During the early years of World War II, few murder cases excited much attention in Britain, which was preoccupied with the large scale tragedy set in motion by Hitler. But in Kenya, East Africa, even the war was eclipsed by a murder mystery that split the British expatriate community.

In that remote and idyllic part of the world, in which modern anthropology has placed the Garden of Eden, social life among British expatriates went on just as before the war — which meant a great deal of big game hunting, social activity, heavy drinking and adultery. One of the most prominently active in all these departments was a handsome — if slightly overweight — aristocrat named Josslyn Hay, who was the twenty-second Earl of Erroll, a Scottish title. Erroll had been expelled from Eton at seventeen, eloped with a married woman to Kenya, then deserted her for an heiress, who died in 1939 of alcoholism. Erroll was a notorious philanderer, and was believed to have slept with every attractive woman in the "Happy Valley" and for miles around.

In November 1940, two more Britons joined the expatriate community: Sir Henry — "Jock" — Delves Broughton, and his lovely young wife Diana. Broughton was thirty-five years her senior, a rather dour, unpopular man who had spent much of his inherited wealth on horses and bridge. In early life he had married well, but his wife's attempts to become a famous hostess had foundered on his unpopularity. When they divorced in 1939, he lost no time in proposing to the aristocratic Diana Caldwell, who rode to hounds, flew her own plane, and ran a Mayfair cocktail bar. He soothed any doubts she might have entertained by assuring her that if she fell in love with a younger man, he would not only grant her a divorce, but would provide her with an income of £5,000 a year.

Diana enjoyed the social life of the Muthaiga Country Club, where she and her husband lived before moving to a farm. But at a Club ball in November, while her husband was away inspecting a farm, she met Lord Erroll, who lost no time in making immoral proposals. After some slight initial resistance, she capitulated, and by the time Broughton returned, his wife was in love with the younger man. Unfortunately, Broughton no longer had the cash to make good his promise of a £5,000 a year allowance — and in any case, no desire to lose a second wife so late in life; he was neurotically afraid of loneliness.

In spite of his shock, Broughton seemed to be taking it very well. On 23 January 1941, he invited his wife, Lord Erroll, and a friend named June Carberry, to a "farewell dinner" at the Muthaiga Club, and toasted the "happy couple". Erroll and Diana left to go dancing, and Broughton's last words to

On September 30, 1906, a young British woman named Madeleine Lake, was found murdered in a wood near Essen, Germany. The money in her purse was still intact, so she was carefully examined for signs of sexual assault. There were none.

Four months later, in February 1907, a twenty-year-old clerk named Alfred Land walked up to a policeman and said he wanted to give himself up for the murder of Madeleine Lake. His story was that he and two companions called Karl and Heinrich had grabbed Madeleine Lake with the idea of sexual assault, but became alarmed after she lost consciousness. All three had run away to Belgium, but he had come back to give himself up. He had no idea of what had happened to the other two.

In court in Essen, he admitted that the two companions were a figment of his imagination. But just as it seemed that a guilty verdict was absolutely certain, a woman who kept a café at Essen where Land always took his meals, insisted that he was there both at lunchtime and in the evening at about 7.30. She proved the date by an entry in an account book. Her two daughters supported her story.

Land's sister told how he had attempted suicide after their father died of tuberculosis and alcoholism. She said that her brother was also an alcoholic. He had been in prison a number of times for fraud.

So, in spite of his protests that he was guilty and wanted to be executed, Land was found Not Guilty.

The evidence suggests that Land had made a false confession to a murder he did not commit out of a desire for notoriety.

But the killer of Madeleine Lake was never caught.

Erroll were to ask him to make sure Diana was home by 3 a.m. In fact, Erroll brought her home by 2.30, accompanied her to the front door, then drove off.

Half an hour later, two blacks driving a milk truck were blinded by headlights blazing through the falling rain, and saw a car tilted over at an angle in a drainage trench. They peered in through the window and saw a man — a soldier — who was obviously dead.

The police were called, and at 8 that morning, a pathologist named Geoffrey Timms was passing by when he saw the "accident". He stopped and ordered the body to be taken out of the car — it had to be dragged out, since the foot was stuck under the accelerator. He then recognized the dead soldier as Lord Erroll. But it was not until the body was taken to the mortuary, and a wound in the left ear washed, that he realized that Erroll had been shot. A .32 bullet was found embedded in his brain.

By now, the car had been towed away, and the removal of the body meant that vital clues had probably been lost. Heavy rain in the night had washed away tyre marks or footprints.

The obvious suspect was Broughton. He claimed to have spent the night in bed, except for two occasions — at 2 o'clock and 3.30 — when he knocked on the bedroom door of June Carberry "to check that she was all right".

Obviously, he could have left the house between these two visits, but there was absolutely no evidence that he had.

Superintendent Arthur Poppy, in charge of the case, knew Broughton, and thought that he was probably capable of the murder. When he heard that Broughton had been engaged in target practice at a nearby farm, he sent detectives to try and find samples of the bullets and spent cases; they found .32 bullets that matched the one found in Erroll's brain and another discovered in the car. Poppy's theory was that Broughton had sneaked out of the house while Erroll was saying goodbye to Diana, and hidden himself in his car. He had waited until Erroll slowed down, then shot him in the ear, hanging onto the safety straps — which were torn out — as the car crashed into the ditch. Then he had returned home and climbed in through a window.

On the morning after the murder, Broughton had set fire to the rubbish in the rubbish pit in his garden, sprinkling it with petrol; later, the remains of a golf stocking, with traces of what looked like blood, were found in the pit. Poppy also found a pair of burnt gym shoes, and theorized that Broughton had worn these to do the murder. He was inclined to believe that the crime was premeditated, since Broughton had reported the theft of two .32 Colt revolvers three days before Erroll's death.

Broughton was arrested on 10 March 1941, and his trial began on 26 May. But although the prosecution case looked watertight, it foundered on the fact that the gun that had killed Erroll had five right hand grooves and a black powder propellant, while the stolen Colts would have had six grooves. The bullets found at the firing range failed to strengthen the case, since the gun that fired them could not be produced. In any case, there was no definite evidence that Broughton had fired these bullets.

So on 1 July 1941, Sir Jock Delves Broughton was found not guilty, and celebrated his acquittal with a dinner at the

Muthaiga Club (as a consequence of which he was deprived of his membership). But life stubbornly refused to return to normal. Ostracized by his neighbours, Broughton decided to go to Ceylon; reluctantly, Diana went with him. Later that year, when he rented Erroll's house, the "Djinn Palace", their relationship became increasingly strained, and she frequently accused him of Erroll's murder; finally they separated.

Broughton returned to England in 1942, and was immediately arrested by the Fraud Squad. In 1938, he had been the victim of two mysterious robberies, both of which had brought him large — and much needed — sums in insurance compensation. The "Broughton pearls" had been stolen from Diana's car on the Côte d"Azur, and later that year, his home had been burgled, and three valuable paintings stolen. Many years later, Broughton's friend Hugh Dickinson was to admit that he had carried out both thefts at Broughton's request.

The Fraud Squad failed to make the charges stick, and Broughton was released for lack of evidence. But his son Evelyn had by now discovered that Broughton had defrauded the estate and cheated him out of the bulk of his inheritance. Broughton's depression increased, and on 2 December 1942, three months after his return to England, he committed suicide at the Adelphi Hotel in Liverpool with a lethal dose of Medinal.

When the author James Fox studied the case in order to write a book, *White Mischief*, he learned that Broughton had, in fact, confessed to killing Erroll. He had made his confession to a horse dealer named Alan Horne. According to Broughton, he had planned the murder of Erroll in association with a man he called "Derek", and he and "Derek" had paid an African £1,000 to kill Erroll.

In 1979, June Carberry's daughter Juanita, who had been fifteen at the time of the murder, admitted that Broughton had confessed to her on the day after the murder. He told her that after killing Joss Erroll, he had thrown the gun into the Thika Falls — he was afraid that the police had seen him do it. "I felt very protective of him after that," Juanita told James Fox, adding that the murder had been a spontaneous outburst of violence and misery because he could not bear to lose Diana.

It seems, then, that the devious Sir Delves lied to the end. The theft of the Colts seems to indicate that he planned the murder. And the story about "Derek" proves that, even when he had decided to "confess", his natural deviousness made him incapable of telling the whole truth.

Jack the Stripper

Since World War II, there have been only two unsolved murder cases in the United Kingdom which rate inclusion in most encyclopaedias of crime. The first, the "Thames Nude Murders", was a series of prostitute-killings in the mid-1960s, so called because the victims were left naked, most of them close to the river. The killer, who became known as Jack the Stripper, was apparently a deviant with a taste for oral sex. The last four victims had traces of spray paint on their bodies, indicating that they had been kept in or near a paint-spray shop. In early 1965, a solution of the case seemed imminent when the police identified the shop as one on an industrial estate in west London. It seemed almost certain that the killer was a van driver who worked at night, and who had access to the shop. The suspect, a forty-five-year-old man, committed suicide, leaving a note saying that he was "unable to stand the strain any longer". The identity of Jack the Stripper has never been revealed.

The Lower Quinton Witchcraft Murder

Charles Walton was practically retired from labouring by the spring of 1945. He had worked on the local farms all his life and now, in his seventy-fourth year, was afflicted with crippling rheumatism. Despite this, he still insisted on doing some work around farmer Albert Potter's farm when the weather allowed him.

St Valentine's Day, 14 February 1945, was a clear and sunny day in Lower Quinton when Charles Walton took up his walking stick and made for Meon Hill on Potter's farm

Many husbands in the Happy Valley must have smiled grimly to hear of Joss Erroll's death. For all his charm, he was a thoroughly detestable individual: good-looking, arrogant, and a dedicated seducer of other men's wives. It gave him particular pleasure to seduce the wives of men who regarded him as a friend – one of his favourite remarks was "To hell with husbands" – and then to borrow money from the cuckolded spouse. He was a bully who treated his servants abominably. He loved humiliating women, and enjoyed the sense of power it gave him to know he had slept with every attractive woman in the "white highlands". He once shocked a friend by saying to a child in a hotel lobby, "Come to daddy", when the child's legal father was within earshot. He also liked to say that he divided women into three categories: "droopers, boopers and super-boopers". There was not a man in the Muthaiga Club who was not longing to see him get his come-uppance.

to do some hedge cutting. Walton lived with his niece Edith who had a war job in a nearby factory. When she got home at 6 o'clock that evening, her uncle had not returned. Normally he was back from work around 4. Edith was anxious, worried that he had fallen and, unable to stand up, was lying out in the open in the approaching darkness.

Co-opting a neighbour to help her search, Edith made for Potter's farm. Accompanied by the farmer, Edith and her neighbour hunted through the fields by torchlight. Their shouts brought no reply. Edith was beginning to fear for her uncle's life. Suddenly, in the beam of the torch, they saw a body. Charles Walton was pinned to the ground with his own pitchfork. Edith, stunned with shock, returned to her cottage escorted by the neighbour while Potter remained with the body.

Only when the police arrived with spotlights did it become clear how violently Walton had been butchered. His throat was slashed with his own hand scythe, which had been left jutting from the wound. His arms were criss-crossed with cuts where he had evidently tried to defend himself. The pitchfork that fixed him to the ground took two policemen to remove – Potter had tried and failed. Cut into the wrinkled skin of Walton's neck and chest was a cross.

Superintendent Robert Fabian, known as Fabian of the Yard, one of Britain's most celebrated detectives, took over the case after local police failed to uncover any leads. A tin watch had been removed from the corpse, and Fabian enlisted the help of the Royal Engineers equipped with mine detectors to search the surrounding countryside for it. Meanwhile, constables took statements from the village's 493 inhabitants.

The crime should have been easy to solve. The murderer must have been someone with a grudge against Walton. In a small community, such a motive would be difficult to hide. This was the rational view. The terrible violence of the attack and the superstitious silence of the locals suggested a more ritualistic cause for Walton's death.

The pinning of a witch to the ground in order to destroy her power is a ritual dating from Anglo-Saxon times. The villagers tacitly implied that this is what happened to Walton. In 1875, a man called John Haywood had murdered an old lady named Ann Turner because he believed her to be a witch who was persecuting him. In his statement to the court he said that it was common knowledge that most of the misfortunes suffered by the local community were inflicted by a small coven of witches. He had merely taken his revenge. He had stabbed her with a pitchfork and cut a cross into her neck.

Fabian uncovered only one other lead. A villager had made a statement to the effect that a POW from the nearby camp was seen wiping blood from his hands in a ditch on the day of the killing. The camp inmates were all searched and an Italian was found to have bloodstains on his coat. He refused to answer questions. The coat was sent, along with other samples taken from villagers, to the forensic lab. The Royal Engineers were despatched to search the ditch. They found metal. It was not however the tin watch, but a rabbit snare. The blood on the coat also proved to be that of a rabbit. The POW had declined to talk because he was scared that he would be punished for poaching.

There the investigation ended — it remained one of Fabian's few total failures. But in their book *Perfect Murder*, Bernard Taylor and Stephen Knight claim to have learned the solution to the mystery. In "The Mysterious Death of Charles Walton", Knight alleges that Fabian was certain of the identity of the killer, but simply lacked the evidence to prosecute. The murderer, Knight says, was Farmer Potter himself. His motive had nothing to do with ridding the countryside of a witch, but was purely financial. Walton was an obsessive saver, and he had lent Potter a large sum when Potter was on the brink of ruin. The money became due; Potter was unable to pay it back, and on that St Valentine's Day, he chose a violent solution to his problem. Potter may not have intended to kill Charles Walton when he went to talk to him about the debt — or to ask for an extension. Perhaps Walton threatened him with court action, or flourished the receipt under his nose. Whatever the reason, Potter killed the frail old man, then mutilated the body to suggest a witchcraft connection.

Knight's evidence for this theory tends to centre upon Potter's conflicting statements to police and the ease with which he found Walton's body in the dark that February evening. His attempts to pull the pitchfork from Walton's chest were, according to the theory, attempts to cover his fingerprints from the time of the murder.

Whether or not Potter killed Walton, the aspect of the story that intrigues is the idea of a well hidden group of Satan worshippers at the heart of a seemingly tranquil English village life. Even if Potter did kill Charles Walton and mark the body with pagan symbolism, where did he learn the pagan symbolism? It would seem that the more comfortable, greed-based explanation of Charles Walton's murder merely leads to more questions.

The Gatton Mystery

Near Brisbane, Australia, in 1898, two girls named Norah and Ellen Murphy, together with their brother Michael, set out for a dance on Boxing Day, and failed to return home. Their bodies were found the next day in a paddock near Gatton; both girls had been raped and battered to death. Convicts were suspected of the crime but it was never solved.

Two years earlier, in 1896, another rape case had made headlines, but the girl had survived. Sixteen-year-old

Mary Jane Hicks made the mistake of accepting a lift from a Sydney cabman, who tried to "take liberties" with her. A group of youths interrupted the attempted seduction and persuaded her to go with them. Three of them also tried to assault her, and her screams brought two would-be rescuers. But they were overwhelmed by a gang of eighteen hooligans — known as the "Waterloo Push" — who soon overpowered them. One of the rescuers ran to the nearest police station. But by the time mounted policemen arrived, the girl had been forcibly raped by a dozen gang members. Six hours later, several members of the gang were in custody. In New South Wales at that time, the penalty for rape was death. Eleven gang members and the cab driver, Charles Sweetman, were charged. Public indignation was tremendous, and nine of the eleven were found guilty and sentenced to death. Eventually, only four were hanged. The cabman Sweetman was sentenced to two floggings and fourteen years hard labour. The savagery of the sentences is an indication of the Victorian horror of sex crime — the feeling that it was something that had to be stopped at all costs. Even the later revelation that Mary had not been a virgin, and had not protested when the cabman tried to "take liberties", made no difference. "Victorian morality" took the sternest possible view of such matters.

The Kidnapping of Charley Ross

The word kidnap, meaning to "nap" (or nab) a child, came into use in the late seventeenth century, when homeless children were nabbed and sold to the plantations in North America. But the first case of kidnapping, in our modern sense of the word (to seize someone for ransom), occurred in Philadelphia in 1874.

Unsolved Crimes

Charley and Walter Ross, four and six years old respectively, disappeared from their suburban Philadelphia home on 1 July, 1874. Walter was soon home again, recovered by a Mr Henry Peacock who had found him crying loudly in front of a downtown sweet shop. Walter's story was, for the period, a strange one. For the past four days, two men had been driving past the front lawn of the Ross's stone mansion and offering the children sweets. On the fourth day, Walter had suggested that they go into Philadelphia to buy some fireworks for the approaching Independence Day celebrations. The two men readily agreed, and took the children to "Aunt Susie's", a sweet shop on the corner of Palmer and Richmond street. Walter was given twenty-five cents to spend and gleefully ran into the shop. When he came out the carriage had gone.

The idea that Charley had been kidnapped did not at the time seem plausible. In fact the crime was not really established as existing; Pennsylvania had no specific law against it. The other reason why extortion seemed unlikely was that despite owning a large stone house, Christian Ross, the boy's father was only moderately wealthy. He had made his money in selling groceries but had recently gone bankrupt. At the time of the abduction he was only just beginning to break even again.

Then, on 3 July, a note from the kidnappers arrived. It was hand-written and only semi-literate. Despite the uneducated appearance of the spelling and grammar, the style was florid: ". . . if any aproch is made to his hidin place that is the signil for his instant anihilation. if you regard his lif puts no one to search for him yu money can fetch him out alive an no other existin powers . . ." The note demanded money without stating an amount, or specifying a method of payment. It was obvious that the kidnappers wished to bargain.

Ross gave the letter to the police and they made the contents public. The community was outraged in a way that perhaps is no longer imaginable. When the police decided to closely search the whole local area, the inhabitants voluntarily allowed officers to search their homes, something that the police would have had legal difficulty in compelling them to do. Anyone who refused the police entry was looked upon with suspicion. Although the child was not found, a great deal of stolen property was, and prosecutions followed.

Three days after the last another note arrived, demanding $20,000 and threatening to kill the child if any detectives were set on their trail. Ross was directed to enter a personal ad in *The Philadelphia Ledger* when he was ready to negotiate. It was decided that the longer an exchange of notes could be maintained, the better the chance of forcing the kidnappers into a blunder. Therefore the ad read: "Ross will come to terms to the best of his ability."

A reply soon arrived, saying that the abductors were getting very impatient, and that the reason for the evasive reply was obvious to them. Despite this Ross continued to publish ambiguous answers. In fact, he had made up his mind not to compound a felony by paying the criminals, and went as far as to announce the fact publicly. This in effect severed the link of communication with the kidnappers and put Charley Ross' life in a great deal of danger.

Seeing that the worry of this situation was driving his wife into an early grave, Ross relented. Through the small ads he signalled his willingness to hand over the money. Shortly another note arrived, remonstrating with Ross for behaving so recklessly and postponing any deal. The reason given was that the phase of the moon was not propitious for business transactions.

On 30 July the instructions arrived at last. Ross was to put the money in a white painted suitcase and board the night train to New York with it. For the entire journey he was to stand on the rear platform of the last carriage, looking back down the track. He was to throw the suitcase off the train at the signal of a torch. It was clear that the kidnappers had been waiting for a moonless night, in order to avoid being followed.

Ross complied, and waited for the whole journey without receiving a signal. On his return a note awaited him, chiding him for failing to keep the deal. It seemed that the kidnappers had read a newpaper report "revealing" that Ross intended to go with the police to follow up a clue somewhere entirely different. Consequently, they themselves had not taken the trouble to turn up. Even if the kidnappers had got hold of the case, they would have found that it contained only a letter demanding a simultaneous exchange of money for child. Ross now communicated this demand to the kidnappers. They replied that simultaneous transfer was impossible, and again threatened to kill the child.

Meanwhile the New York police had found an informer capable of identifying the handwriting of the ransom notes. According to this man the writing belonged to a William Mosher. The informant said that a few years previously, Mosher and a man named Joseph Douglas had approached him to be an accomplice in abduction of a millionaire's child. The information seemed promising, and the police traced Mosher to 235 Monroe Street, Philadelphia where he lived with his family. Douglas lived in the same house. Unfortunately, by the time police searched the building the Moshers and Douglas had moved to New York.

At about the same time a final communication reached Ross. It instructed him to place an ad in *The New York Herald* reading "Saul of Tarsus: Fifth Avenue Hotel", followed by the date that he would be there with the money. Ross did as he was told, sat in the hotel all of 15 November, but there was no visitation. The kidnappers remained silent.

On 14 December, the summer home of a Mr Van Brunt situated on the Upper East Side of New York was burgled. Mr Van Brunt was in residence, and heard the intruders climbing down into his cellar over the sounds of a storm. By the time that the burglars re-emerged from the cellar, there were five armed men waiting for them. Mr Van Brunt shouted "Halt!" The burglars fired two shots, both of which missed, and tried to escape out of the window. Van Brunt shot the nearest man with his shotgun, nearly blowing him in half, while his son jumped on the other burglar and accidentally shot him through the chest with a handgun. It was clear that both men were dying. Although in terrible pain, the burglar with the chest wound refused to be moved, and asked for an umbrella to keep himself dry during his last moments. In between fits of pain the man spoke: "Men, I won't lie to you. My name is Joseph Douglas and the man over there is William Mosher. He lives in New York, and I have no home. I am a single man and have no relatives except for a brother and a sister whom I have not seen for twenty years. Mosher is married and has four children" (here pain for a moment overcame his speech). "I have forty dollars in my pocket that I made honestly. Bury me with that." After another fit he continued: "Men, I am dying now and it's no use lying. Mosher and I stole Charley Ross." Van Brunt asked him why they had done it. "To make money." was the simple reply. When asked where the boy was Douglas told them to ask Mosher. He was told that Mosher was already dead, and his blasted body was dragged over in order to prove it. Douglas said that they had known that the police had them cornered. All he would say about Charley was that: "the child will be returned home safe and sound in a few days." Douglas survived over an hour of agony in the rain. Eventually he lapsed into unconsciousness and died.

The bodies were taken to the morgue, where a terrified Walter Ross identified them as the men who had taken

Charley. Despite Douglas' dying assurances, and a reward of $5,000 and no questions asked for anyone who returned the child, Charley was never seen again.

Mr Ross carried on searching for his child, heartened by a statement made by William Westervelt, Mosher's brother-in-law and the man with whom Mosher and Douglas had lived in New York. He had told Ross that the day before he died, Mosher had said that he would arrange a simultaneous transfer if that was the only way to get the money. This pre-supposes that the boy was still alive.

Westervelt was tried as an accomplice in New York, and despite a lack of any firm evidence, he was sentenced to seven years in solitary confinement.

It has to be assumed, despite Westervelt's statement, that Charley Ross was dead long before Mosher and Douglas were shot. Perhaps he was killed when Christian Ross announced publicly that he had no intention of aiding a felon. An unconfirmed story reports that Charley Ross was delivered into Westervelt's hands almost immediately after his kidnap, Mosher and Douglas remaining in Philadelphia to arrange ransom notes and payment. Westervelt, according to the story, became nervous and drowned the child in the East River. This was impossible to confirm however, as Westervelt disappeared after serving his sentence.

Christian Ross spent the rest of his life and his money checking up reports of Charley, travelling as far afield as Europe.

On 25 February 1875, Pennsylvania Legislature officially recognized kidnapping as a crime.

The Mystery of Amy Robsart

Queen Elizabeth I herself may have been party to a murder. Her lover, Sir Robert Dudley, (later the Earl of

Leicester), was an extremely handsome but thoroughly spoilt and undisciplined character. When he was only seventeen, he had married Amy Robsart, the daughter of Sir John Robsart, a Norfolk squire — apparently they married for love, and remained in love for some years. But Dudley became involved in the conspiracy to make Lady Jane Grey queen of England. It failed, and Dudley's father, the Earl of Warwick, was executed for his part in it. Dudley was also sentenced to death, and his wife had to visit him in the Tower of London. However, he was pardoned, and redeemed himself by fighting against the French at the Battle of St Quentin (1557). When Elizabeth came to the throne in the following year, Dudley lost no time in hurrying to court, where the twenty-five-year-old queen became violently infatuated with him. Soon he had been appointed Master of the Queen's Horse and made a Knight of the Garter. The Spanish Ambassador wrote to Philip of Spain to tell him that Robert Dudley would probably be king in the near future.

Two years later, in 1560, the Dudleys moved to Cumnor Place, near Abingdon, Oxfordshire. On 4 September of that year, Queen Elizabeth told a foreign envoy that Amy Robsart was dying — an odd statement in view of the fact that she seems to have been in normal health, and apparently on excellent terms with her husband.

Four days later, on 8 September, 1560, Amy is said to have sent all the servants to Abingdon Fair — her husband was at court. When they returned, they found her body at the foot of the stairs with a fractured skull. Apparently she had slipped on the stairs. The coroner's jury found her death to be accidental. And as the relations between Robert Dudley and the Queen became closer, rumours abounded that Dudley had had his wife murdered, with the Queen's connivance. The actual killer was rumoured to be Sir Anthony Forster, Dudley's

Comptroller of the Household at Cumnor, in association with his mistress, Mrs Oddingsells.

For whatever reason, the Queen decided not to marry Dudley. He was probably her lover anyway (although historians deny this), and she had no desire to share power with a husband. She even tried to marry Dudley off to Mary Queen of Scots, but he declined. In 1564, Dudley was created Earl of Leicester.

In 1575, Dudley laid on the famous entertainment for the Queen at Kenilworth Castle, an entertainment described at length by Sir Walter Scott in his novel of that name. The eleven-year-old Shakespeare is said to have witnessed it. But Scott goes on to take some major liberties with English history. He makes Dudley marry Amy secretly, and a villain called Varney later arranges her murder by means of a booby trap outside her bedroom door.

Was Amy murdered? The historian Ian Aird argues that her death was an accident, due to the cancer of the breast from which she is known to have been suffering. But the Simancas Archives indicate that there was a plot to poison Amy, and this may be what the Queen had in mind when she said that Amy was dying. On the other hand, she may merely have known about the cancer of the breast.

Dudley's future career was not particularly glorious, but at least he escaped execution — the fate of Elizabeth's other favourite, the Earl of Essex. When the English went to help the Dutch against the Spanish in 1586, Dudley proved arrogant and incompetent as their commander, and returned home in virtual disgrace. But he had one more triumph — he stage-managed the Queen's famous visit to her troops at Tilbury — when the Spanish Armada was on its way — when she made her famous speech describing herself as "a weak and feeble woman", but with "the heart and stomach of a king". A few months later, in August 1588, Dudley was dead, at the age of fifty-five, of a "burning fever".

Whether or not Dudley planned the murder of his wife, there seems no doubt that he was one of the most unpleasant and treacherous characters in English history. When Mary Queen of Scots was in prison in 1587, Dudley tried to persuade the Queen to have her quietly poisoned. And with the evidence of a poison plot against Amy in the Simanca Archive, it seems more than likely that her death was no accident.

The Peasenhall Mystery

1 June, 1902, was a bright, sunny morning after a night of storm. William Harsent, a carter, walked through the peaceful Suffolk village of Peasenhall, on his way to take clean linen to his daughter Rose. He walked through the wet garden of Providence House, where the girl was in service, and pushed open the back door. What he saw made him drop the linen. Rose Harsent lay, half naked, at the foot of the stairs. Her throat was cut from ear to ear, and deep gashes covered her bare shoulders. She had been wearing a nightdress, but this had been partly torn from her, and partly burnt away. A broken medicine bottle lay on the floor beside the body.

The local policeman arrived, followed by the doctor. The policeman discovered that the broken medicine bottle had contained paraffin — which had apparently been used in the attempt to burn her. The girl's bed had not been slept in, but there were three letters in the room, one of which made an appointment to come and see her at midnight.

The signature made it clear that the author was William Gardiner, a young foreman carpenter who lived nearby; he had a wife and six children, and was known as a devout Methodist. Medical examination revealed that Rose Harsent had been dead at least four hours, and that she had been pregnant.

The great American *cause célèbre* of 1904 was the trial of *Floradora* girl Nan Patterson for the murder of her lover Caesar Young in a hansom cab. The shot that killed gambler Caesar Young was fired at about 8 o'clock on the morning of 4 June, 1904; he was dead by the time he reached hospital. Nan Patterson claimed he committed suicide but the police disbelieved her – to begin with, the revolver was in Young's pocket, and it seemed unlikely he would have placed it there after shooting himself.

Young, who was married, had met Nan Patterson on a train to California two years earlier. It was a passionate affair, but by 1904, Young wanted to terminate it; to that end he booked passage for Europe for himself and his wife on the *Germanic*. He and Nan spent a last evening quarrelling violently. He nevertheless met her for a breakfast of brandy and whiskey, after which they called the hansom, and Young was shot soon after. Under the circumstances, Nan's story that he killed himself because he was upset about leaving her seemed unlikely – the bullet had entered at the wrong angle. At her first trial, a juror became ill, so a mis-trial was declared. Her second trial ended with a hung jury. When the third trial also ended in deadlock, all charges against her were dropped. In retrospect it seems clear that Nan was acquitted, not because she was innocent, but because the men on the jury felt she was too pretty to hang.

Nan cashed in her notoriety by accepting leading roles in various musicals, but proved to lack talent, and soon vanished into obscurity.

No one had any doubt that the father of the unborn child was William Gardiner, for in the previous year he and Rose had been the subject of scandal in Peasenhall. Two youths had seen them walking towards an empty cottage known as the "Doctor's Chapel", which stood alone in a field. The youths had hidden behind a hedge until the two had gone inside, then crept closer. They were unable to see what was happening, but the sounds made it clear. There was a rustling of clothes, then the girl gasped "Oh, oh."

The silence that followed seemed to suggest a state of mutual satisfaction. Gardiner was heard to ask her what she was thinking. She answered: "What you were reading last Sunday." He asked her what he had been reading, and she replied: "About what we are doing now." She then went on to quote the verses from Genesis, chapter 38, about how Onan "spilled his seed on the ground".

When the story was repeated in Peasenhall, the villagers, who knew their Bible, had no doubt that Gardiner and Rose Harsent had either been engaged in extremely intimate "petting", or that the youths had overheard an act of *coitus interruptus*. Gardiner was a Sunday School teacher; Rose Harsent was one of his choir girls.

The scandal was so great that an enquiry had been conducted by the Reverend John Grey; Gardiner had denied the story, saying that he had been in the "chapel" with the girl only to help her move a stiff door. Gardiner had been told "Let this be a warning to you for life", and had appeared to be suitably chastened. Yet although he promised to have nothing further to do with the girl, it was plain to people who observed them closely that they were still on intimate terms.

The day after Rose Harsent's body was found, a superintendent of police called on Gardiner, and asked him if the handwriting on one of the letters was his; Gardiner denied it. The policeman asked if the envelope in which a certain letter was contained was not identical with those used by Gardiner's building firm; again he denied it. But the next day, he was arrested and charged with Rose's murder.

Certainly, the case against him looked black. His clasp knife was found to be stained with blood, although he claimed he had been cutting up rabbits: in 1902, there was no way of testing whether a bloodstain was from a human being or an animal; Paul Uhlenhuth *had* discovered the basic principle in 1900, but it had never been used outside Germany.

Various witnesses said that they saw a large fire burning at the back of Gardiner's house on the morning after the murder; the prosecution argued that this explained why no bloodstained clothing was found in the house; Gardiner's wife testified that there had been a fire, but that it was only the usual fire they lit on Sundays; but she did not explain why they needed a fire on a hot June morning.

Gardiner's defence was an alibi, supported by his wife; he said he had been at home all evening, and been in bed beside his wife all night. Gardiner was lucky. In those days the jury's verdict in a murder trial had to be unanimous, and one member of the jury stubbornly refused to be convinced of his guilt. The judge had to order a retrial, and once again the jury failed to agree.

Gardiner should have been tried a third time; but the authorities decided he had been through enough, and entered a *nolle prosequi* – which meant no further prosecution would take place. It was equivalent to the Scottish verdict of "not proven". Gardiner and his wife moved to a

London suburb, where they opened a shop. Whether they prospered or not has never been recorded.

Was Gardiner guilty? We can never know. Certainly, Gardiner was not the only man who might have made Rose pregnant. Highly indecent verses were found in her room, and proved to have been written by the youth next door, who was in love with her. She was no blushing wallflower, but a forthright country girl who had no objection to keeping obscene verses. She may well have had other lovers beside Gardiner — a solution adopted by Brian Cooper in *Genesis 38* his novel about the murder, which suggests that the dissenting jury man who saved Gardiner's neck at the first trial knew the identity of the real murderer.

Only one thing is clear: Gardiner came close to the gallows, not because the evidence against him was particularly strong, but because the jury found it hard to forget that this Sunday School teacher had misbehaved himself on the floor of a disused cottage with one of his choir girls.

Titles in the World Famous series

World Famous Cults and Fanatics

World Famous Scandals

World Famous Strange Tales and Weird Mysteries

World Famous Crimes of Passion

World Famous Unsolved Crimes

World Famous Catastrophes

Future titles
in the World Famous series